PERFECT BALANCE

AQUIL ABDULLAH

with

Chris Ingraham

Potomac Sculling Publishing

Printed by
Signature Book Printing
www.sbpbooks.com

Potomac Sculling Publishing
Copyright © 2001 by Chris Ingraham

First Edition November, 2001.
ISBN: 0-9710 865-0-8

Technical Advisor: Byron Derringer / **www.digitalfuturephotography.com**
Technical Advisor: George Kirschbaum / **george@thecoxguide.com**
Graphic Design: Aleksandr Gembinski / **www.alek.org**
Cover Photo: Chris Milliman / **The Independent Rowing News**
Quotations from Henley Royal Regatta are credited to:
www.total.rowing.org.uk/hrrlive.html

Additional copies of PERFECT BALANCE can be purchased online at **www.rowersalmanac.com** or by writing directly to:

Potomac Sculling Publishing
4043 Mansion Drive, N.W.
Washington, D.C. 20007
potomacsculling@aol.com

Potomac
Sculling
Publishing

Acknowledgements

I would like to thank my family, my coaches, my fellow athletes and those people everywhere who so generously support athletes like myself with their time, advice, financial aid and personal support. Without them this dream would have been impossible. A special thanks goes to Dean Maxwell for asking me, "What do we win when we don't win?" after my loss at the 2000 Olympic trials. His question was truly the first step of this book's journey.

To Kay Mickel, Mohmoud Abdullah and Merrill McKenzie

Table of Contents

Introduction

In this book I will tell my story. Like any story, it may mean different things to each reader. The rowing world is a small and tightly knit community. Those readers who know rowing will understand the importance attached to events like the World Championships or the National Team Trials. They will understand the enormity of difference between the Dad Vail Championships and the Eastern Sprints in college competition. To others, for whom rowing enters the scene only in Olympic years — and then with passing curiosity — the events rowers dream about have much less significance. How each type of reader responds to this book may be quite different.

For just under a decade, I have given my life to rowing. I have struggled to compete among those select few people who are the best oarsmen on the entire planet. Of all the bodies of water that cover our blue earth, only a handful of people can row a shell over them as quickly as this elite group. We aspire for the claim of being the best there is, and not just every four years when the Olympics are on TV. Our quest is daily. It begins with the rising sun and the morning fog that lifts from a placid river or lake. It goes on in the afternoon when we hit the water for another workout, in the heat of the summer sun, or the wintry hints of late autumn dusk. At work, at dinner, in bed, it infiltrates our dreams — watery, gliding dreams — until with the dawn the quest begins all over again. Every year, elite oarsmen from around the world compete in the World Championships to see who can prove themselves as the best. This title has never been mine, though I've been close, and though I continue every day to try.

Sometimes I think of how far I still have ahead. The weight of so much effort, time and exertion tumbles down on me, and I want to give up. But I can't give up. My story is not valuable because I have decided to pursue a dream. It may not be valuable because of what success I have achieved, and certainly not because I am somehow unique in coming so close to a goal then falling short. Many great athletes and people have missed their aims after spending years trying to reach them. In this I am not special. Let this also remain clear: my journey as an African-American man competing in a historically white sport has not been the fairy tale of an impoverished and troubled soul overcoming great adversity to reach the top. We all face adversity. Mine has involved less racial and social obstacles than most people who pick up this book might suppose.

With *Perfect Balance* I want only to share one man's personal struggle to be the best in a sport, and to find meaning from efforts that repeatedly fall shy of their mark. In sports, as with life, the moments when I have seen things with perfect clarity have not lasted for very long. I have known seconds of stability, and brief pockets in time when the boat disappears, the oars fade away, and I am in *perfect balance*. But the majority of my life has been spent on either the left or the right of the balance scale. Nothing lasts forever. No longer do I not look at defeat as a failure, or at adversity as a hardship. Instead I search for meaning in my actions and try to understand what drives my decisions. If things don't go as planned, I have learned to make new plans, or to work harder, in order that they might go better next time.

This story is no how-to guide for finding perfect balance. It tells of an individual in constant struggle to achieve that balance for himself. I hope, if this book does anything at all, it will inspire its readers to make their own honest self-search. Such has been my journey, and the friends and lessons I've gained along the way are enough to have made all my endeavors worth trying. It may sound familiar, but in this great world, no struggle is in vain. As easy as it can be to forget sometimes, nothing is forever, neither victory nor defeat.

CHAPTER 1

My First Worst Defeat

In June of 1999, when I arrived at the Henley Bridge, which overlooks the great gray river Thames to the north and south, I paused to gaze down along the water, and at the course I hoped to conquer in the next couple of days. Looking downstream, to my right I saw Leander Boat Club. Immediately past Leander sat the boat enclosure and grandstand, the seats for the hundreds of pilgrims who had traveled to this rowing Mecca of Henley-on-Thames. As I peered down the left bank of the river, I could see the banners of crews that were lucky enough to be housed near the finish line. There was no actual line, not that I could see, yet it hovered there in my mind, somewhere over the water between two small white towers. I visualized crossing it in the days ahead.

Here was the Henley Royal Regatta, crew's most illustrious event. Other regattas were larger, maybe even better tests of an oarsman's talents than the Henley, but none had the same prestige. Since 1839, barring only eleven years during the two World Wars, the Oxfordshire town of Henley-on-Thames has held the annual event for crew's elite competitors.

That year at the regatta's 150th anniversary, I would participate as a single sculler in my first elite international race. Along the banks of the river stood vacant folding chairs, joined in the shadows of the overcast day by large white tents following the curve of the water's edge. The plastic chairs and canvas tents glistened under a gentle rain, and the river flowed quickly beneath the falling drops. Rain or not, on race day we would be rowing against the current. The course would be difficult, I thought. My work would be hard.

That afternoon was the last before the regatta began, and it seemed to have frozen under the tranquil silence of the drizzling sky. Though the rain was hardly burdensome, only a few people moved about outside: stewards, caterers and a few crews. The caterers disappeared with tall stacks of plates under the shelter of a tent, then emerged moments later holding something new. In under twenty-four hours, the empty chairs, the lonely tents and the silent river would fill and overflow with people who emerged from their seclusion indoors.

Every one of the approximately 420 competitors from around the world, racing in the 17 events held over the next five days, had trained strenuously to be there. I personally had logged at least 3,000 miles on the water that year, many with Jamie Koven, the other American representative in the single scull. Despite the diversity of our backgrounds, we all came with a common goal: to win. Of course, only a select few of us could win, and whoever those winners were would be told by the week's end. From the time I arrived on the bridge to the moment before my first race, I was nearly too excited to wait.

On race day, the starting platform was eerily quiet. I paddled slowly to my place, noted how the Thames smelled more pungent than the Potomac back home, how the water felt more buoyant under my boat, and how the banks cupped the river with a different embrace than what I'd seen before. Maybe I was just nervous. My opponent was nervous too. We were quiet, mesmerized by the tradition that surrounded us.

I raced against, in Henley parlance, "Van Den Brock, Castledore Rowing Club." Prior to the race, I had tried to obtain an idea of his speed by asking some of the local oarsmen, but all they could tell me was, "Well, he's pretty fast." This came as no comfort. In my first elite international competition, there were only a few names I knew with certainty. Van Den Brock was not one of them, but that was no guarantee of his weakness. How did I compare? We sized each other up from our boats. We smiled quickly then resumed our stolid faces of focus. *Must seem tough. Must intimidate.* I recalled the instinctual rules of competition. Neither of us could allow our internal doubts or nerves to make an external appearance, otherwise the mental race would be lost before the real race began. Our gravity of mood carried over to the people holding our boats from the platforms. They didn't say a word while watching the official. We too sustained our silence, poised in position while watching for the signal to begin.

In his navy blue sports coat and spotless white trousers, the official stood in his boat with solemn face, focused on his task. My fingers gripped the oars, arms outstretched. Since arriving earlier that week, my focus had been strong. I could think of nothing but starting that first race. Although I had the support of other members of the U.S. contingent, of Jamie Koven's coach Scott Roop, and of Boyd Lytle from Resolute Racing Shells, I was otherwise at the regatta alone. There had been a few details to sort out regarding my boat, and I had practiced with Jamie for a brief time the day before, but other than that I was left to endure the dreadful waiting by myself. When finally aligned at the starting platform and ready to perform, the official seemed the ideal figure to bring all my anticipation to its breaking point. He held his arm to give the sign. My mind focused inward. *Do this, Aquil. Make it happen.* With the drop of the flag and the sound of the horn, we were off.

I was off. The person staking Van Den Brock's boat held his vessel from starting. As I pulled away my opponent stayed behind. *Was this it? Was it going to be this easy?* Still rowing, my eyes turned toward the official in the boat. He motioned for me to proceed if I so chose. My eyes turned back to Van Den Brock, struggling, desperate. I recalled all my feelings of anticipation and excitement. He must have felt the same. I could not go on, not like that. I stopped rowing and signaled to the official that I wished to restart the race. With his obliging nod, I backed water and returned to the starting platform to begin the race again.

Unlike most races in which I've participated, the Royal Henley Regatta holds races in single rounds of elimination, pitting competitors one-on-one. Two wooden booms indicate the oarsmen's course, and the only thing between the shells is four feet of water. This head-to-head format enabled us to start again conveniently. When we repositioned ourselves, our lanes remained the same. I rowed the Bucks lane, he in the Berks. Berkshire and Buckingham counties lay on opposite sides of the river, hence the names attributed to either lane. The closeness of the two paths have through history seen many rowers disqualified for clashing oars with a competitor, or for rowing outside their designated space. Stewards were poised to follow us down the course in magnificent wooden powerboats. They would enforce the rules. As for the ruling of the starting official, he said I could have proceeded to race ahead of Van Den Brock. But that was not my style. The faulty start at the outset was a product of everyone being antsy on the first day of the regatta. There should be another chance.

When the official gave his signal again, this time we went off without incident. The stewards followed along, careful not to obstruct us with their boat's wake. I made sure to stay in line between the booms, paying close attention to navigation. *Hard port. Easy Starboard. Steady. Steady.* To pull out over the water, oars dipping and turning, body sliding, back stretching, felt as if a valve had been released inside my head and the pressure of the preceding days hissed out into the quiet Henley air. I lost myself to the task at hand, gliding down course until I glanced to my side and realized, about halfway through the race, that the victory was easily mine.

What a relief to finish that first race! My confidence before the race had not been poor, but I didn't realize until finishing how anxious I had been. After that first victory, all my jitters disappeared. With the first and most mentally agonizing race over, it occurred to me for the first time where I was and what I was there to accomplish. *Whew!* What a long way I had come.

Only a few months earlier I was sitting in the third quad in Augusta, Georgia, trying to earn a spot in the quadruple sculls for the 1999 World Championships. When my efforts in Augusta left me shy of my goal, I had to determine what to do next. It could feasibly have been the end of my rowing career. Instead I decided to pack up from Augusta and head to Boston, to push myself that extra bit further. Of all the advice I solicited from rowing friends and family members, Jamie Koven, the 1997 world single sculling champion, made the most convincing case. He suggested I race internationally at Henley and Lucerne to test my skills against rowers from outside the United States. He then put me in touch with the National Rowing Foundation and Knickerbocker Management, so I could resolve the practical concerns required to make it happen.

By the time I arrived at Henley, I had been through my best season of competitions in the single, but had no outstanding medals to show for it. Here, on the Thames, I would have another opportunity to compete. The composed faces at the starting line never betraying their confidence, the silence over the water on race day perfect and calm — these things drew me back to competition. I could never leave the sport, could never stop competing to be the best, to test myself. After a disappointing year of training for the World Championships, it pleased me that the U.S. National Team Trials were not my final race of the summer.

Thanks to a rowing friend named Dan Debonis, I was able to obtain accommodations with Mark and Justine Lewis, two Henley residents. Mark had spent some time rowing with the New York Athletic Club, and someone from the club put Dan in touch with Mark. The Lewis's were kind enough not only to host me, but to host Dan and Will Fisher, as well. Dan and Will were competing together in the double sculls, and they brooded over their first round race against the powerful U.S. double of Ian McGowan and Nick Peterson. We all tried to endure the wait between races, knowing that we soon would be on the water, responsible for making or breaking our own success. The humidity of the summer had peeled the paint away from my oars, and I gladly took to painting the blades to occupy my mind.

On the day of my second race the scene amazed me. Before it had been calm and vacant, then with an instant snap it filled with action. Tents covering 12,800 square feet swarmed with people and food. Caterers worked busily with all they had to provide: one and a half tons of Lobster, 8,000 bottles of wine, 900 kilograms of smoked salmon, 3,000 duck breasts, 500 kilograms of beef, 1,000 loaves of bread, one and a half tons of strawberries, 5,000 scones, 4,000 bottles of champagne and another 4,000 pints of Pimm's. Rumors suggested that Britain's Princess Royal was or would soon be in attendance. She had last attended in 1988, and before that in 1977, so it was no small deal to have her watching. In fact, it was a huge deal, not just to have her there, but to be a part of the whole spectacle, to see the men in their navy blazers and straw hats, and the women primped in their finest sundresses and bonnets. Even the other crews made the atmosphere tense with excitement, and given the unique format, with only one race at a time, two boats in each race, all eyes would be on me.

Without all this hoopla, my first race against Van Den Brock seemed in retrospect to be anti-climactic. All my nervous energy had spilled into the strength of my stroke, and a few minutes later I had emerged victorious. My second race, on the regatta's third day, was different. My victory over Van Den Brock meant that I would be racing Richard Briscoe from Leander in the second round of the Diamond Sculls Challenge. Briscoe was a local favorite who had competed at the elite level in the past. His prior success gave rise to some concern, but my previous race had gone so well that I had enough confidence to overcome what concerns I had. I was ready to take care of business. Before my race against Briscoe, my training partner Jamie Koven won his second race in the same event, meaning that if I beat

Briscoe then I would go head-to-head with my rowing inspiration and close friend in the next day's semi-final race.

On the river again, the water did not smell so strange, the surface did not seem so oddly buoyant and the hug of the riverbanks was not as abrupt. The water kept a swift current beneath us, and I was ready, after a night spent visualizing my victory, to begin the race with a fresh and strong start. We rowed to the starting point and aligned the bows of our boats. I waited for the signal. Waited. Bam! My legs fired forward. Arms low, chin up, reach, slide, catch, fire with the legs. My first two strokes were solid. With the third, my legs fired forward and my foot-stretcher, bearing the full pressure of my legs, broke from its hold. At that moment my mind seemed to break from its hold as well. *This couldn't be the end!* As was custom, the official gave Briscoe the chance to continue. I looked desperately to my side, and like I had done yesterday for Van Den Brock, Richard Briscoe stopped rowing so I could start over with him at an even keel. After near disaster, I would have another chance.

I rowed to a small dock near the starting line while Briscoe rowed to the line itself. Quickly I tried to fix my foot-stretcher. Never in my life had I screwed a wing nut so tight. When I was satisfied with the board's sturdiness within the hull, I motioned that I was ready again. This time there would be no coming back. With the same austere motion as before, the official signaled our beginning, and again my legs fired against the foot-stretcher. It felt good. My start was strong and the boat slid over the water as I pushed each oar blade just under the surface. One stroke, two strokes, three strokes. I was on my way. With each successive push of the legs my confidence built and the strength surged, propelling me backwards toward that finish line I'd visualized so many times before.

Briscoe and I were even. A dozen strokes in, I felt great. Thirteen, fourteen, still fine. But on the fifteenth stroke, the problem returned. *No, this wasn't right.* My foot-stretcher *was* on securely. I'd seen to it myself. The metal support bar jiggled; the wing nuts loosened. The board fell free of the hull. There was nothing for me to do. Briscoe didn't stop. My race was ruined.

When I look back over my rowing career, there are many moments that stand out above the rest, some good, others bad. In terms of defeat, I don't imagine one can ever feel more distraught than I did during the 1999 Henley Royal Regatta. There I was, thousands of miles from home, stuck idle on a river while my opponent cruised to victory behind me. Hundreds were watching, and in expectation of a match against my friend and training partner Jamie, I sensed disappointment in the crowd when they learned the match would not occur. No matter how great their disappointment, mine was far the greater. I had built high expectations for my first season of racing in Europe, but in my debut, all I could do was bow my head in utter defeat.

       ✿   ✿   ✿   ✿   ✿

    Even with all my defeats, many people have told me that my story is inspirational. They say I am a pioneer because it is so different, unique and challenging for an African-American man to participate in a sport with a primarily Caucasian tradition. People have compared me to Jackie Robinson, the first African-American person to break the color barrier in professional baseball. The truth is, there have been other people of color who have competed among the rowing elite long before I came to the sport. Most notable is Anita DeFrantz, who has been an Olympian, and now sits as Vice-President of the International Olympic Committee. Outside America the list is too large to record. Countries like Egypt and Cuba have great rowers of color. Nevertheless, people in black and white communities remind me that I have forged new possibilities for African-Americans in the sport of rowing. As best I can, I try to downplay any such praise. My involvement in crew is not some nursery tale about a downtrodden athlete who has overcome great adversities related to the color of his skin. The crew world has embraced me as its own without regard for the color beneath my racing jersey. I like to believe that any respect and admiration I have received were earned through human qualities that transcend racial distinctions. Jackie Robinson's quest was far more hindered by prejudice. He lived in a different era and, aside from the social differences, my story differs from Jackie Robinson's in another respect: I am not the best at what I do. I have fallen short of my goals time and again. Yes, my decision to row may be monumental insofar as I am the first African-American man to compete at the elite level of an overwhelmingly white sport. And yes, the blades of subtle prejudices that minorities face every day have, at times, nicked me. But these slights are not the norm in my life, and the most important parts of my story are not what I have learned through my struggles with racism.

    Regardless of ethnicity or race, I am a simple individual who has learned that one has to work hard to get where one hopes to arrive.

Perhaps this is no great lesson. We will never be the best we can be until we work as hard as we can and push ourselves to a limit we create every single day. We must repeatedly set our goals and gauge our performance to form new goals that tightrope between realism and ambition. Somewhere between the easy objective and the impossible objective is a useful, balanced, alternative. To find the appropriate goal requires a great deal of awareness — awareness of oneself, of others, of one's limitations and obstacles. After that it only remains to work hard. This story is one of discovering who I am and testing what my limits might be, not just as a black man in a white sport, but also as an individual who, like many others, strives to succeed.

CHAPTER 2

The Starting Line

It never occurred to me to think that I should or should not do something because not many people of my skin color had done it before. My upbringing in Washington, DC does not have horror stories of struggling to find a meal or fending off drug dealers outside the stoop of a housing project. I have always been provided for and taken care of with a modest but sufficient middle class lifestyle. Growing up, I participated in those things that seemed most enjoyable. I played football, hockey and golf, to name a few, and I never made much note of the racial makeup of those around me. My parents encouraged me to do what I wanted so long as I worked hard at what I did. For a while, all I wanted was a challenge and some exercise. My father pushed me to make sure I had both. He would race me up hills, destroy me in basketball and chastise me if he saw me quitting. From the beginning of my involvement in athletics, my interest was always in the activity itself, in the competition and its exhilaration. What mattered most were human values, not lessons pertaining to one race vying against another.

By the time I got to Woodrow Wilson High School, I was a young man of many interests. Football was my favorite sport, and I had dreams of playing in College, but there was little I wouldn't try. Many of my friends rowed and urged me to give it a chance, but in my sophomore year, in addition to football, I started playing golf in the spring, leaving no time for crew. As the years went by, football remained my focus. After my senior football season, the coach at North Carolina A & T expressed an interest in bringing me to his school on a football scholarship. This had been a goal of mine for a long time, but I was beginning to wonder how much I really wanted to play college football. In order to improve my running speed, the coach suggested I run track. I had no particular aversion to track, but I still considered golf my spring sport. Meanwhile my friends Ben Eaglin and Aaron Gordon continued trying to convince me to row. Ben was the coxswain on the Wilson team, and Aaron was the captain. They could probably sense that I was bound to try crew sooner or later. If I hadn't tried rowing then, as a senior, chances are good that I would have never tried it. It's funny to see in retrospect how my priorities could easily have sided with golf or track. Either one would have kept me on the path I was already on. But something about rowing drew me toward the water. I cannot say whether it was my friends' powers to convince, or something less quantifiable, but at seventeen, I picked up an oar for the first time.

Deciding to row was an interesting cultural experience for me. It was the first time that I was in a predominantly white environment. Golf and my brief stint with hockey as a child gave me glimpses of this, but rowing had a different feeling. There was something academic about crew, something about oarsmen with the "golden boy" mystique. To oarsmen, the sport itself was what mattered most — increasing fitness, perfecting the stroke and rowing fast. I may have stood out in a boat of eight as the only black man in a line of white rowers, but I was only judged by the same criterion as everyone else. How well did I account for my share of the workload? How hard was I trying? These questions mattered more than my skin color.

Part of my development as a person has involved a journey through many different views on race and racism. Today, I still believe what I sensed back with the Wilson crew. Seldom are the times my rowing companions have made me feel alienated or unfairly judged because of my "difference." Growing up, that difference never seemed like anything to fuss over. My parents always strove to place me in multicultural situations, and when I was younger I didn't understand why some black people hated white people, why some white people hated black people, or why anyone hated anyone else. It wasn't until my teen years that I first noticed that not everyone shared my naive and idealist attitude.

Tiny injustices based on my skin color would accrue in the everyday parts of my life. For example, when I went into a store, the store's employees would often trail me thinking that I was scheming to shoplift. Other times I would stand outside and try to hail a taxi, only to watch cabs drive right by me and pick up white passengers further down the street. Would these things have happened to me if I had been a white teenager? Perhaps. Or perhaps I was just reading the situation incorrectly. I tried to give everyone the benefit of the doubt, but I still found cause for anger.

Once when I was fourteen I was walking with a friend named Pascal Foley. At the time, Washington, DC was the "Murder Capital of the Nation." As a young black man I felt guilty until proven innocent. We were walking Pascal's dog in upper NW Washington, DC — an affluent and pleasant area — minding our own business and squirting each other with a water gun. Suddenly ten police officers jumped out of patrol cars, guns drawn. As we later learned, an under cover policeman had seen us playing with the water gun as he drove by. Prey to the fears that must linger in the back of any police officer's mind in a city grown notorious for its violence, the cop thought we were threatening to shoot him. He called for backup, and when we reached the corner of the street, a team of police aiming 9mm guns at our heads screamed at us to drop to the ground. We obeyed, and when they found out that the gun was a toy, they yelled at us (almost disappointedly) and told us to go home. There was no apology. Most of the officers were white, but the undercover officer who had called for backup was black. The stereotype equating black teenagers to "dangerous menaces" was so pervasive as to affect even a black officer who was once a black teenager like myself. Didn't he remember what it was like? He had grown up when times were even worse for minorities. I was not looking for trouble or doing anything disruptive. Yet, even he had acquired a sense of judgement based on skin color. Since then I can't help but wonder what the officer in the car would have thought if we had been two young white boys walking a dog under the same circumstances. For the first time in my life I became very aware that America viewed me as dangerous solely because of the color of my skin.

It didn't take much more than those episodes for the situation to anger me. Teenage anger can take many forms — angst, rebellion, reclusion. I kept my anger inside at first, as mere frustrations I would have to explore further. The frustrations penned up inside me too long, until they teetered close to bitterness and needed to be released. I began to exhibit small signs of paranoia, and could not help but think that the first thing "white America" noticed about me was that I was black, not that I was fat, or skinny, or had a wooden leg. Reading books by Malcolm X, Marcus Garvey and W.E.B. Du Bois only fed my aggression. Suddenly I began to look at things in terms of black and white, foolishly believing there were an "Us" and a "Them." My frustrations could no longer remain inside. With the unbridled aggression of a teenager I started talking about "The Man," and I bought into the belief that my life would be a struggle against a white America that only wanted to hold me down.

Many of my mother and father's friends were white, which posed serious issues for my young mind. Was it okay to hang out with white people? Did that mean they would think I accepted all the injustices I'd noticed? Was it okay to have both white and black friends? That I enjoyed the company of most family friends only made my views on race more confusing. From the age of fourteen to seventeen I struggled profoundly with who I was and where I belonged in the world. Every teenager undergoes a phase of stress and self-discovery in these formative years, but at the time I didn't have such perspective. The struggle to find my identity in a world of so many conflicting messages wore me down. Racial issues were at the heart of everything I did. Most of my friends were black, but rowing as a high school senior turned that around. I began to get a fuller sense of myself and the diverse world around me.

In high school I began crew by sweeping in a boat of eight with a group of novice underclassmen. Cultural issues slipped from my mind when I discovered with amazement the power and balance required to move a boat gracefully across the water. Rowing in the Washington spring air and around the beautiful landscape of the Potomac River affected me far beyond any issues of race. I had found a new love, a love for a sport segregated not by law, not be intention, but by the preconceptions people had about the sport. I was hooked immediately. But despite my newfound passion, doubts of my acceptance still lingered.

One day, I think I was sixteen or seventeen, after watching the evening news my frustration about the question of race in America put me in a particularly ornery mood. There was crime everywhere, and so many people presumed black people were the guilty ones. When would the stereotypes end? Forget all this fawning. If people were going to judge me, then I was going to judge them back. I had a heated argument with my mother. How could she not see what was wrong? Or how could she see it and take it so calmly? If she didn't understand then she was part of the problem. My temper was hot. She looked at me as if she didn't know me from Adam. The person I loved most, with whom I wanted the most kinship, seemed completely distant. It made me realize how venomous hate had made me. Until our quarrel, I don't think that my mother ever knew how deeply I had fallen into believing that my struggle in this life was against white America. As I stood there in rage, she said to me, "Aquil, how can you be for the freedom of one people and against the freedom of another? Isn't freedom for one freedom for all?" The conversation ended when I walked out of the house. It occurred to me while walking the streets of Georgetown, that hatred does not lead to communication, and lack of communication leads to no resolution. I decided then and there to take another approach to dealing with my feelings about race and racism.

All I could do was be myself. If I wanted others to accept me as a human being and not just as a black man, then I too had to accept people as human beings. Pleased with this new philosophy, I began to do things because I wanted to do them. As I had done as a child, I made choices without thinking twice about the color of anyone's skin. From that point, however, my choices were not made with childish naivete, but with the knowledge that irrational notions like "Us" and "Them" have no constructive part in making the world a better place. The prejudices that were visible in so many places had not disappeared; nor had I chosen to ignore them. Rather, I felt liberated with the knowledge that I need not respond to forms of prejudice and oppression by oppressing others in the same way. I felt free at last. When the time came to hit the water and row, I did so with great devotion.

By April, the head rowing coach at The George Washington University, Paul Wilkins, approached me with a half-tuition scholarship for rowing at GW. The opportunity had arrived after I'd already been accepted to colleges elsewhere. Coach Wilkins told me that if I acted quickly, I still had time to submit an application to GW. At the time, George Washington University was one of the few universities that offered scholarships for rowing. It was an opportunity I could not pass up. Shortly after that I submitted my application. I was accepted, and some serious thinking remained.

Where should I go to college? Throughout the rowing season that year I stayed in contact with the football coaches from North Carolina A&T. They sent me information about summer practice and instructed me on when I needed to arrive for camp. For years the football scholarship would have been my top choice, without pause, but now with the prospect of rowing at GW, I didn't know what to do. After finding rowing so enjoyable, and having taken to it relatively quickly, it would have been hard to leave it in favor of a moderate chance at football greatness in North Carolina. All my life I had hoped to play football in college, and GW did not have a football team. The decision was no easy one for a seventeen year old boy, and my mind changed every day.

One day, late in May of that year, some friends and I were preparing a week long trip to the beach. We were all set to go when my mother pulled me aside and said, "You're not going anywhere until you decide where you're going to college." The pressure stumped me. My friends waited outside eager for the sand and sun, and I sat in my kitchen under my mother's scrutinizing eyes, trying my best to make the decision that would shape my future.

With a casualness that I think surprised us both, I said, "I guess I'll row." My mother nodded her head and I went outdoors to hit the waves.

❊   ❊   ❊   ❊   ❊

The decision to continue rowing in college kept me involved in the sport at a time when I could easily have let it leave my life. Being a collegiate athlete posed new challenges I had not faced in the past. Learning time management skills and how to balance my various commitments became a painfully apparent necessity during the first semester of my freshman year.

In the summer before entering GW, I participated in a program run by the school's Multicultural Student Service Center (MSSC). In the program I was able to take a sociology course for full academic credit, and I was also able to meet other students with backgrounds similar to my own. The sociology class came easily to me, and I aced it with little difficulty (a feat that would later save me when my other class work began to slide). It was socially where the MSSC afforded the greatest opportunity. Like most incoming freshman, I was eager to meet new people and establish a network of friends. I was just beginning to overcome some of the foolish anxiety that plagued me through high school. An environment of extreme cultural diversity was the perfect place to do it.

Around this time, I met two people who exerted a large influence on my early college years. James Cheeks and Allen Johnson were incredibly talented people who shared my interest in playing music. I had played the saxophone for several years and always thought I was a fairly good musician. Then I met James and Allen, and learned how far I had to go. They were so far ahead of me in their understanding of music that I was sometimes embarrassed to play with them. That summer, whenever we weren't participating in other activities, we could be found in the music department practicing. We would each go to different practice rooms and try to play louder and better than the guy to our side. Musically, I had a lot of catching up to do, so I devoted a huge portion of my time to the sax. By the end of the summer it paid off. Our group was asked to play at a school function. Before long, one function led to another, and soon I was heavily committed.

Toward the end of the summer I met David Marsh, who was a Professor of Music at George Washington. He asked if I would like to play in the Latin Ensemble. I told him that I would be more than happy, when time permitted. Little did I know that I was setting myself up to be spread too thin. David Marsh was a taskmaster and he required us to play every song to perfection. For me, that meant a lot of practice. Playing music and taking one class in the summer is easy enough. When the academic year began that fall and I had to row, go to class, play music and (of course) attend every social engagement that crossed my way, I quickly fell behind in school. Neglecting my work or performing poorly in it had never been a problem before. Juggling my various activities became difficult when hours whizzed by in front of a video game console, or listening to music, or seeking the affections of a lovely girl. Setting priorities was crucial. Unfortunately, choosing which commitments to favor did not come easily because I loved so many different endeavors. My academic pursuits fell to the bottom of the list. By the end of my first semester, my performance in the classroom needed some serious assistance. I first sensed trouble when I could only answer one question on my physics final. When I slept through my calculus exam, I knew for sure that I had slipped too far.

Shortly thereafter, my mother received my grades in the mail. When she picked me up for Christmas break, she waited until I entered the car before slamming me with her maternal tirade. She ended the rant by saying she refused to pay half-tuition and other expenses for me to get drunk and chase women, so if that was what I wanted to do, then I better find a job. Her point made, I fell silent. No longer was I the angry teenager ready to quarrel when someone didn't see things my way. Besides, she was right. She turned the key in the ignition and we drove home. Until I left for the GW rowing camp in Florida, I remained in my room studying. Nothing else was said.

Upon returning to school, I decided to make some changes that would help me balance my time more productively and get the most out of my activities. I moved into a new dorm where the video game black hole and the constant procrastination would not be as problematic. My new roommate, Ben Adams, made a difference as well. Ben was a transfer from Lehigh University, in his junior year of school. We had met through rowing. Ben's father, Terry Adams, was a National Team oarsman who had competed in the '70s and early '80s. Aside from being an easy and amicable person to live with, watching how Ben handled his various obligations helped me to do a better job of coping with mine. From Ben I learned how to do all of the things that I loved as well as get all of my schoolwork done.

Another change I made that second semester was to meet weekly with Sheila Hobin, the guru of academic support for intercollegiate athletes at GW. Sheila was one of those rare people in the world who is so kind that I could not bear to let her down. She ensured that I attended study hall; she looked over all of my assignments; and she made sure that I met with my professors once a week. Thanks to her help (and my refusal to disappoint her) I made the Dean's List in the spring semester of 1992. I was starting to find a better balance after making only a few key adjustments. The adjustments themselves were not extraordinary. I still managed time to meet women and play a video game or two. Rowing hadn't dropped off and I hadn't closeted my saxophone. Being around people who helped me attain a more lucid sense of priorities made the difference between having too much on my plate and just the right amount. Ben Adams and Sheila Hobin helped me focus, respectively, on rowing and academics. The other interests filled in the gaps, and before long I noticed that finding a balance not only gave me more time, but it gave me the wherewithal to approach my endeavors more fervently. Now that everything was more manageable, I approached things with a more serious attitude — especially rowing.

Training for rowing has never been a big ordeal for me. I just do it and try to leave everything at the boathouse when it's finished. Sometimes my energy wanes and other times my enthusiasm needs some stoking, but my philosophy has always been to concentrate on what I am doing when I am doing it, then move on to the next task after I'm done. That spring my training took a higher intensity than it had in the past. Although Paul Wilkins recruited me, I wound up rowing for John Devlin. John had previously coached the women at Georgetown and he was an all around winner. He strengthened the rowing program at GW by creating a competitive atmosphere where only the best could survive. Many athletes who thought they were good were soon pushed to the side. John placed a premium on fitness. One of the guys on my team, Matt Russell, was one of the team's strongest members, but he had to lose some weight. John put him up to the task of losing it, and he did. Each of us had our own challenges to face. Mine, like most of the other oarsmen's tasks, was to train at the level necessary to be the best in our league. Those who stuck with it, like Matt and myself, turned out to be solid oarsmen under Coach Devlin.

Without Coach Devlin inspiring us to maximize our potential, we would not have had much success. The team's talent was decent, but in order to be really good we had to match up with other crews, in both strength and technique. My freshman year, the average ergometer score of the Varsity eight for a 2000 meter test was somewhere around 6:25. Crews in the upper echelon of collegiate rowing had average erg scores approaching six minutes. This meant that in terms of raw power output, we would sometimes be up against over a twenty-second difference in the course of a race. The ergometer, or erg, is a grounded rowing machine designed to gauge an oarsman's strength, stroke rating and speed moving a boat. Coach Devlin knew, and reminded us, that we would never improve our erg scores if we didn't train harder and with a smarter agenda. His reminders taught me just how crucial it is to practice with good habits and to work hard. The expression "practice makes perfect" suddenly seemed inadequate. Instead I started to think, "only perfect practice makes perfect."

During that first year at George Washington University, I learned the difference between excelling on natural talent and improving through hard work. Some people can coast by through life on natural athleticism or intelligence. Others are not so fortunate. I could not control what effort others put in to their quest for their dreams. Nor could I have any say in what natural talent God had given me. All I could do was find the balance in my responsibilities and thereby increase my energy and seriousness. Once I had the verve and focus, I could channel my God given attributes toward whatever I wanted to accomplish. If I increased my training efforts, then I could build on whatever natural talent I possessed to become an extremely competent rower. When I realized this, not only did I learn of my true potential, but I learned of the potential we all have to succeed in life if we make a concerted effort to practice wisely, prioritize our goals and work rigorously to accomplish them.

During the fall of my freshman year at GW, Coach Devlin had put me in the Junior Varsity eight, also known as the 2V. The eight is a boat of eight rowers, each with one oar, and a coxswain who steers the boat. By the spring of that year I was in the Varsity boat with one other freshman named Tim Downs. He rowed in the stroke seat of the Varsity eight and I rowed in the two seat. The boat's stroke is the oarsman seated at the stern, who sets the pace for the other rowers watching from behind. The stroke is usually one of the boat's strongest rowers; it's up to him to set a high standard of exertion. Tim had a lot of talent to start with, and he did a good job. Together we nurtured grand ideas of making GW the greatest collegiate crew around. We vowed that we would make the GW crew one to reckon with by the time we were sophomores.

College life was good. After conquering troubles with time management, I took everything as it came, and I coped with it well. Socially I operated in many different circles, but as rowing began to receive most of my attention, I spent more time with my rowing friends. One day I went to the movies with some friends on the team. We went to Union Station in Washington, DC, and all around us were black people. Suddenly I felt uncomfortable. There I was among white peers, having fun, when all the worries of my younger years came back. Why was I hanging out with all of these white guys? Where were all my black friends? At school I didn't have many black friends at all. There were some friends I had met at the MSSC before school started, but by this stage most of my buddies were white rowers. Things were so good before, in a multicultural environment, but now I felt like I'd forgotten all about those times and hadn't even noticed I was doing it. I felt that I was losing touch with my Afro-American heritage. I felt like a sellout.

Although everything had been going well, the experience at Union Station made me feel like an outsider looking in on a life I once lived. I saw some of my black friends from high school, and they gave me strange looks after seeing me with all these new white guys. For a while I tried to pretend that I wasn't with my rowing buddies, but it was too obvious to conceal. When did I become so alienated from the people of my race? Confusion coursed through my mind, and I acted awkward and aloof, as if I had to choose one set of friends over another. What do all my black acquaintances think of me now? I wondered. Am I giving them the wrong impression? What impression did I want to give? Issues that I thought I had resolved years before came tumbling back upon me, and once again, I suffered the doubt of a man not sure where he belongs.

Being a sellout is a concern I imagine many black people who live in predominately white environments must face. While wanting to remain true to my identity as a black man, living among white peers made it difficult. My closest friends were white, and our friendships had nothing to do with skin color. Our relationships were founded on the same principles of camaraderie, trust and compatibility as any close friendship I'd shared with black people. Yet still I was uneasy and could not ascertain a reason why. The white buddies I had were genuine. I was not the "token" black friend in their lives. I was just a friend, regardless of racial difference. Maybe I felt such an intense tendency to split my friends down racial lines because I still had lingering notions of "Us" and "Them" in my mind. With black people I had a shared cultural identity. There were similarities that united us simply because of our common experience growing up as American minorities. Associating with these people made sense and felt natural. It gave me a sense of solidarity. At Union Station, when I noticed the dearth of black acquaintances in my everyday social group, I felt something close to the opposite of solidarity. I felt weak, like I had betrayed other people of black skin.

Fortunately, I had matured enough during that year to impede any harmful attitude before it took its hold. Others would have had no reason to suspect anything was wrong. The Aquil Abdullah on the outside seemed to have everything together. My schoolwork had improved. My rowing was at its best. The social life I lived left no vacancies for complaint. But on the inside, a lot of confusion still lingered. How to best deal with it, I didn't know. I couldn't just abandon my white friends in favor of black ones. Even if I could, it wouldn't have been what I wanted. Somehow I had to find a better balance. I took a job at the MSSC, to force myself into a multicultural environment.

Being back at the MSSC gave me a chance to feel comfortable again by giving me the sense that I was staying in touch with my roots. Spending time with people of color and of various cultural backgrounds helped me work out some of the issues that troubled me. For instance, jumping back and forth between different racial environments showed me that people really accepted me based on the quality of my character, not on the color of my skin. More importantly, I found people were more similar than I had given them credit for. The thing to do, I decided, was to look at the world without so many polarities. I need not have *only* black friends, or *only* white friends. Both were possible, even if the interests of each group did not show much overlap. The process of understanding these lessons and integrating them into a way of life took some time. Slowly, I made my way.

Then, just as my thoughts were becoming clear, just as my insides were piecing together with my outside, something happened that sent me spinning once more in the all too familiar cyclone of doubt. My cousin went to jail for shooting a man who later died from the gunshot wound.

My cousin's name is Jonathan Carle, and we were close friends when we were kids. Perhaps because of our closeness, or because I realized how easily I could have gone in the same direction as he, his imprisonment had a deep impact on me. With only a few changes of details, I imagined it could have been me in his place. It scared me that someone so close at heart could have done something so terrible. All the racial stereotypes that I'd spent so much time refuting suddenly seemed to make more sense. I remembered the black police officer who had thought Pascal Foley and I were threatening him with the water gun. The officer had probably seen too many kids like my cousin Jonathan. Maybe young and black really did mean "dangerous menace." It was frustrating to have, in my own family, so accessible an example of the racial stereotype supporting itself. After recently experiencing positive interracial interaction with the rowing team and at the MSSC, there came a real visceral reminder that not all people have the quality of character to function in a world of so many different people and agendas. I'd just started to feel satisfied with a romanticized humanist view, but now I had to question it all over again. How could others judge me by my character when someone so close to me, someone with my own blood, had committed such a horrendous act? How different could I be? Whereas before the racial struggle had affected me through incidents I always dismissed as the ignorance of select strangers, now it hit so close to home that I felt myself a part of the problem.

As children, Jonathan and I were companions at play. He had a violent stepfather who was a strict disciplinarian. I didn't like going over to Jonathan's house when his stepfather was around, but in other times we were as close as two young boys can be. Jonathan has always been tough, street smart and athletic. We were often in competition. Each wanted to beat the other in a sport, or impress the other with a remarkable feat. Our friendship was strong and healthy for a time, but in junior high we went in separate directions.

Jonathan began to hang around with a different crowd, the kind that frequently got in trouble. His grades dropped, and his other more productive interests fell to the wayside. As an impressionable youngster, of course, it was precisely this time when I began to envy him the most. When I was a child I was never really a tough kid and never really "in" with the popular crowd. My two best friends in junior high, Sam Bonds and DeLante Jackson, were by my standards two of the coolest guys I knew. We walked our own way and never really followed anyone else. Jonathan's coolness had an entirely different feeling. It came with a forbidden sense of danger, of risk. Whenever I had the chance to hang out with my cousin, I would find myself in situations that weren't very wholesome. We would throw eggs off the top of buildings at traffic on the street below. We would throw things at people on the bus, and we would push over transvestites in their high-heeled shoes. Nearly everything we did got us in trouble. To me, all these adventures were exciting. I was playing the rebel. But the kid who everyone thought was so good was doing things that weren't so good at all.

When we started high school, eggs turned to guns and drugs. I looked in on Jonathan's dangerous world with a compelling sense of curiosity. Jonathan had all of the privileges that I had growing up, but for some reason he chose to follow the path of a drug dealer. I am not sure when he decided that criminal behavior was his only option in life, but I know that after the death of our grandmother there was a certain sadness about him that I could never fully understand. Why do kids with plenty of options choose to sell drugs? Neither Jonathan, his friends, nor I came from families for which crime was the only life choice, yet that was what we chose.

I admit to the mysterious appeal of a life of crime. Not only did I make an effort to spend time with Jonathan and his crowd, but I also asked if he would "put me on." That was the parlance used to seek admission into the world of drug running and criminal shenanigans. I wanted to run with the dealers and thugs. The allure of a lifestyle unknown to me had an attraction founded in its potential to relieve my juvenile angers and insecurities. It was an adventure I thought I could handle. By then I had started organized sports and built an identity that was relatively exemplary among my peers. The distance between the worlds that Jonathan and I inhabited had increased rapidly in high school. Fortunately, when I wanted to join Jonathan on his adventures, he knew it was not for me. "Aquil," he said. "You don't want this."

Of course he was right. I didn't want it at all. What I really wanted was acceptance, for him to think that the privilege of my upbringing and the straight-laced All-American quality of my actions were okay. Jonathan was a good guy; he just thought that criminal activity was what would make him a man. It was hard to fault him when I believed the same thing. I wanted to be respected, I wanted acceptance, I wanted to be cool, but the truth is that I had no idea of what it meant to be cool. When Jonathan told me I didn't want to be joining his crowd, I realized that he recognized my other options. Why he failed to see that he had other options, too, I will never know. As the years progressed, Jonathan and I did not hang out as much as we did in our earlier childhood. My focus turned to constructive activities like football, golf and eventually rowing. Jonathan went his own direction.

Dealing with my cousin's imprisonment was hard on our whole family, but in many ways we saw it coming. The hardest part was letting go the notion that we could have done something to prevent it. Had we somehow failed Jonathan? It had never been a secret that Jonathan was on a perilous path. Perhaps we could have interceded before he went too far, we thought. In the end, though, it only made sense that we were all responsible for our own actions and that there was not much anyone could have done.

Another hard part of dealing with Jonathan's incarceration was thinking about what people would think of me if they knew that I had a criminal in my family. Would they think that I was a criminal? I felt terrible watching my mother and my aunt, Valerie Davis, cry as the judge handed down Jonathan's sentence. During that time at the end of my freshman year at GW, my family members made an effort to stick together and help each other cope with the situation. We made it through as best we could.

The confusion in my life took a highly introspective turn. Part of me wanted to drop everything and give up. Like many minorities, I spent a great deal of mental and emotional energy trying to debunk the stereotypes that many people hold of my race. What was the point in trying to break down racial barriers when we all end up thinking what we will anyway? No matter how many times I thought about the conflicting ideas in my head, only one conclusion made sense: I had to follow my own agenda, to stick with what I believed. If my beliefs and lifestyle put me in a predominately white world, then so be it. As long as I was being true to myself then I could not go wrong. By looking inward to reach this understanding, I focused on what mattered most in my life. Friends, family and rowing were the immediate things that came to mind. If I chose not to row, or not to socialize with certain people because doing so made me feel like a sellout to the black race, then I was looking at my obligations to the black race incorrectly. A person, it seems to me, can only go through life doing what in his mind is best for himself and for others. I loved my friends. I loved to row. I could go on struggling against the parts of my life that gave me the most fulfillment, or I could surrender to them and live my life in their pursuit. The choice was easy.

Rowing became more enjoyable than ever before. Every day I seemed to improve. The gains I made each day may have been possible because I was in a small program with room for improvement and advancement, but being able to observe my constant progress kept me excited about the sport. Focusing on improving as an oarsman helped me escape from all the personal issues that I was dealing with in other areas of my life. When I was on the water, all I had to do was pull.

By the time my freshman year concluded, I was flying high. All things considered, my second semester at GW had been a stellar one, both on the water and off. My grades were good, my social life was active and my rowing skills were becoming better than ever. Through the encouragement of one of my friends and teammates, Brian Winke, I decided to continue my training over the summer. Brian was by far the strongest rower in GW's program, and when I started to have dreams of making the National Team, it was Brian who put me on to the idea of rowing in the summer. I would soon come to realize that the best rowers in the world trained all year round.

Everything was going well until the night of the year-end rowing party. In a festive revel I punched a hole in a wall and broke my hand. It was a stupid injury, a drunken blunder. Nevertheless, the damage was done. In response to my pleas, doctors were able to rig my cast so I could continue to grip an oar and row. That I even wanted to try such a thing said a lot about my perspective. I was becoming incredibly committed to the sport.

That summer, heeding the recommendation of Brian, I participated in a special summer rowing development program at Potomac Boat Club (PBC), just down the river from Thompson's Boat Center, where crews from both GW and Georgetown were based. Tony Johnson, the head coach at Georgetown, was the coach of the development program at PBC. I asked Tony if I could row sweep for the summer and he told me that he had a lot of good oarsmen coming to row at PBC, and that I was a little on the small side. He suggested that I try the sculling program. Although the seeming demotion upset me, in retrospect it was probably the best change that could have happened. Maybe Tony knew it all along.

Tony Johnson is one of the most interesting coaches in rowing. He stands somewhere around 6'4", with a typical rower's frame, and gray and white hair that earned him the nickname, "The Silver Fox." Most of the time, the Silver Fox is temperate and mild mannered. That entire summer I never saw him lose his cool. He sustained an even manner that carried over to the steady strokes of his athletes. It wasn't until the next summer when I was rowing in the sweep program that I saw the Silver Fox take on the hard edge of a great coach. We had been racing to win seats in the top boat. It was a particularly hot and humid morning on the Potomac. Tony pulled up to our boats after what we thought was the last seat race, and he said something along the lines of, "We are going to stay out here until the same guy wins two pieces." It was hot and we were tired, but we did three more pieces.

When I first began sculling, in the summer of 1992, my performance was not helped by my desire to be sweeping instead. One day, Tony sent me out in a double scull with Brian Elts. We flipped the shell and wound up soaked in the waters of the Potomac. I was pretty frustrated with my early attempts at sculling, but that summer the coach of the sculling program was Alex Machi, and Alex patiently coached me through many bad strokes. My final race of the summer was in the quadruple sculls at U.S. Rowing's Club Nationals. I rowed with David Miller, Frank Lomax and Brian Elts. We didn't come close to winning, but we had a great time. By the end of the summer I was happy that I had learned how to scull, and grateful that Tony had suggested it.

Many new things began for me that summer. In addition to being the first time I tried rowing with two oars instead of one, it was also the first time that I met Jeff Hanna and Greg Johnson, who rowed at Georgetown. Greg was the son of Tony, the Silver Fox. In years to come, Jeff Hanna would become one of my closest friends. Rowing at PBC that summer made me realize that the level of rowing beyond the shores of the Potomac was far greater than I had ever imagined. The summer also gave me the unique experience of realizing again how fortunate and blessed my life had been.

In particular, I learned to appreciate more profoundly some of the people who had played a big influence on my life. I traveled to Alaska with Dr. Merrill McKenzie and his father. Most kids are lucky to have just one father figure in their life, but thanks to Dr. McKenzie, I am lucky enough to have two. Merrill and I have known one another since I was around ten years old. If there was ever anything that I couldn't do because I couldn't afford it, Merrill made sure that money was not the problem. If ever I needed someone to take me somewhere, or to help me out of a tough situation when my parents were not around, Merrill was there for me. When I continued sculling after that summer of training at PBC, it was Merrill who bought me my first single scull. To him I am truly indebted. Our trip to Alaska was incredible. Although it forced me to cut some of my summer rowing short, the time away enabled me to take measure of my year and prepare to have an even better sophomore year ahead. We cruised through Alaska on a luxury cruise ship; we stayed in Denali National Park for a week. In all, I saw parts of Alaska that are more beautiful than anything else I have beheld in my life. If I could have found a way to row and study in Alaska, I may never have returned. But I did return, this time to face what would perhaps be the most defining year in my early rowing career.

Returning to school in the fall of 1992 was a great feeling. I had already been through a year of college, and as a sophomore I was familiar with the college lifestyle. My niche was already carved. Also, the rowing I had done over the summer put me ahead of the oarsmen on the team who had taken the summer months off from the sport. That year we had a couple of new recruits for the team, so we anticipated a strong season. Coach John Devlin could not conceal his excitement for the year ahead, but he knew we had a long way to go.

Intercollegiate rowing is an incredibly competitive sport, with different levels of competition. George Washington is not an upper tier university in the rowing world. When I rowed in college, men's college rowing on the East Coast involved essentially two levels: the Eastern Sprints League, and the Dad Vail League. Today there remain two different levels, but some of the schools formerly considered Dad Vail schools have since moved to what is known as the Champion League.

At the end of the collegiate rowing season there is a championship regatta called the Inter-Collegiate Rowing Association Championships, or the IRA. At the IRA, colleges from both the East and West Coasts compete to see who is the best, but schools from weaker leagues tend to race small boats. The theory in the past, as I understand it, was to have schools race in the Dad Vail League until they were good enough to race in the Eastern Sprints League. Although many of the schools in the Eastern Sprints League are Ivy League schools, Ivy League schools are not the only schools that participate in the Eastern Sprints. George Washington tended to do well in the Dad Vail League, and now GW does well in the Champion League, but the school would likely not be as successful in the Eastern Sprints. Either way, during my sophomore year we knew that the best we could hope for was to maximize our potential. Coach Devlin did everything he could to make that happen.

Thanks to us, Coach Devlin was not alone in his ambition. Tim Downs and I were still determined to make the GW crew one of the best around. As freshman, we had been driving in the bus watching as the final race at the Dad Vail Championships moved down the course along our side. We didn't want to be watching the race; we wanted to be participating. To get there this year a lot of work had to be done.

In college, rowing teams are limited in the number of organized practices that they can conduct. In order to reach the levels we aspired for, our team would have to surpass the acceptable amount of practices. All our extra workouts had to be done on our own, or with a few other oarsmen, unofficially. Rowing at Potomac Boat Club during that summer proceeding my sophomore year helped incredibly. Four George Washington University oarsmen rowed at PBC: Brian Winke, Matt Russell, Perky Gogo and myself. When the intercollegiate season began, we had a distinct advantage.

Brian was still the strongest oarsman on the team. He stood a massive 6'6" and weighed over 220 pounds. He had played basketball in high school, and could outrun almost any person on our team. Brian had all the tools to become a superb oarsman, and in my eyes, he also worked harder than anyone else. Our team would practice at 5:45 a.m., but in the afternoon Brian would return to row on the erg, to lift weights or go for a run. Sometimes he did all three. I decided that if I wanted to be good, then Brian was the guy who I should make my training partner. At this point, I just wanted to do my part in making GW boats go as fast as possible.

Other oarsmen had the same goal in mind, particularly those who rowed with me that summer at PBC. Matt Russell, for instance, was probably the second strongest member of the team my sophomore year. He was a hard working person who would never quit, no matter what the circumstances. Throughout the start of my freshman year Matt was a little overweight and out of shape. Coach Devlin scolded him severely and Matt responded by losing weight over that winter. By the time he returned for my sophomore year, after a summer of developmental rowing at PBC, Matt was in good shape and ready to chase Brian down.

Prospero Gogo, or Perky, as we called him, was the other oarsman who joined us at PBC and made great strides in his ability. Perky was about 5'11" and in the winter of my freshman year he matched me pound for pound at 173. Then in the summer he trimmed down to be a lightweight rower in the summer competitions. Perky was fairly strong, but his technical skills as an oarsman made him stand out. He had been the stroke of the Varsity eight at GW my freshman year, and during my sophomore year, when the season officially began and our sanctioned practices took place, Perky rowed stroke again.

That year we had a strong boat and had become a solid crew in our division. The regular season went well and by the end we took third in the Dad Vail Championships, our national championship at that time. We also took third place in the Champion International Regatta, which was a new regatta that year but also a championship regatta. Our Varsity boat consisted of James Rivera in the cox seat, and, from stroke to bow, Perky Gogo, Dave Kryzwda, Brian Winke, Matt Russell, Alex Mundt, Tony Spinelli, Tim Downs and myself. Each member of the team contributed in his own way, and each one has a special place in my heart.

James was a transfer from the Coast Guard Academy. Despite some shadiness at the start, he turned out to be a good guy. James had the uncanny ability to upset Coach Devlin with the slightest misdemeanor. One morning when James was late to practice, Coach Devlin threatened to quit. Another time, during our winter trip to Tampa, Florida, James split from the group on the beach and we thought we had lost him. Finally, when we were in our van driving down the highway, we saw James running down the road behind us waving to be let inside.

Dave Kryzwda was probably the third strongest guy on the team my sophomore year, trailing only Brian and Matt. Dave and I did not hang out together very often outside of rowing, but he was always at the boathouse and on the water to get the job done.

Alex Mundt was a second year rower, who, like many people in the sport of rowing, did not start until his freshman year in college. On the surface, Alex might strike people as not all together, but as soon as he started speaking, everyone knew differently. Alex was brilliant. He won a Fulbright scholarship and later worked for Ethel Kennedy.

Tony Spinelli, at 6'4", was a baby giant. He had rowed in high school, so when he arrived at GW, he went straight to the Varsity team where he made the Varsity boat. As the youngest member of the team, Tony took the most abuse, but being as big as he was, we knew that we could only push him so far.

Tim Downs was probably one of the best rowers on the team. He rowed in high school at LaSalle in Philadelphia. Since our freshman year, the two of us found our way into many adventures together. Coming to GW from LaSalle must have been a great change for Tim; LaSalle was one of the top rowing schools in the East Coast, and they had won the boys pair at the Royal Henley Regatta in England. Tim and I were probably the only two freshmen who did extra workouts on our own time during our freshman year. We kept that up as sophomores and enjoyed sharing our extremely active imaginations. While we trained, we would imagine ourselves rowing to victory at an international regatta. At the time this was only a joke of our imagination. Little did I know, it would one day become a reality.

To make the finals at the Dad Vail Championship after a mediocre freshman season was a huge accomplishment. We were the first George Washington crew in the Varsity eight to take a medal at the Dad Vail. Thanks to hard work and determination, we really witnessed the George Washington crew undergo a massive improvement. Developmentally, no other year was as important as my sophomore season.

In the summer that followed that year, 1993, I returned to PBC to continue my training. That was the summer that I really got to know Tony Johnson's son, Greg, and Jeff Hanna from Georgetown. Not only did we each enjoy rowing, but we also had a strong friendship away from the water. Such friendships made it easier to endure the difficulties of a grueling training program.

The final race of the summer was the Canadian Henley, and Jeff and I drove up to participate. The adventure began from the start. First Jeff and Greg's pet snapping turtle, Chester, escaped in the station wagon. Not until we were outside of Philadelphia, when we stopped at Jeff's house in Devon, did we find Chester again. That night we stayed at Jeff's house, letting his mother take care of us while we recharged for the long drive ahead. The next day we switched cars and started out for Canada. Before long Jeff tired of driving, so I offered to take the wheel for a couple of hours. The car that we'd picked up at our pit stop had a standard transmission, which I did not have much experience driving. After an hour or so on the road, I mistakenly attempted to shift from third to fifth gear. Jeff claims that I tried to shift into reverse at 50 mph, but I will deny this until my death. One way or another, the car made an unearthly noise and broke down with a putter. We were in Sellings Grove, Pennsylvania. As soon as the first wave of aggravation ended, we phoned AAA roadside service, and the person we spoke with told us that it was a short tow to the mechanic's garage. We waited for a while and finally had the tow truck come only to tow us a few yards away, to the garage that was hidden behind a billboard right next to where we had broken down. After that we figured the car was cursed, so we rented a new one and drove it the remainder of the way to St. Catherines, Ontario.

At the 1993 Canadian Henley I did not make the intermediate eight. Potomac Boat Club, the club I rowed for, had three entries in the intermediate four, but the eight was expected to be the best. Jeff and I were in the same four, and Jeff was also in the eight. We didn't have great expectations for our four. The eight ended up winning, but our four gave a good showing too. We won our first race and advanced to the second round. Our boat was named the Shuttleworth after one of my high school coaches. But the boat was too heavy. I told Coach Johnson and he chuckled, then he said that if we made the final he would get us a better boat. Well, we made the final. Sure enough he made good on his word and in the new boat we took off flying. We led the race for the first 1000 meters, and I remember just blazing down the course. After that, the other Potomac Boat Club boats were too strong, and we fell behind. By the race's end, PBC had placed boats in the first three positions. We weren't first, but it wasn't bad for a trip that started out so cursed.

The school year began shortly after our return home. That summer I had swapped back and forth between sweeping and sculling, but in the fall Coach Devlin suggested I try the single at a race called the Princeton Chase. He let me use his boat for the race, and I managed to run plumb into a log that protruded from the shore. The bow of the boat folded like an accordion. When I returned to the boathouse Coach Devlin couldn't believe his eyes. Maybe the single wasn't the best choice for me after all. From then on Coach Devlin and I would joke about the phantom log that collided with the boat.

It was these sorts of inside jokes that began to give texture to my years as an upperclassman at GW. Meanwhile I continued with school and kept on rowing. The racial and social turmoil that bothered me before had subsided to a level I could handle. Having finally found a balance between my social life, my music, my job at the MSSC, my academic work and rowing, it felt nice to look upon the incoming students with an upperclassman's experience and authority. Now I was the one advising people on how to manage time. The leadership position was less conferred than something gradually stepped into by all of the older rowers who had been in the program. From the new perspective of an older student, everything was a bit changed. Brian Winke had graduated, along with a few other guys who had been in the Varsity boat. The younger oarsmen looked up to us, as we had to our superiors. We tried to be exemplary, but most of the time we just did what we normally did — worked hard on the water, played hard off it. Although we hoped that the crew that year would be as strong as the previous one, it did not measure up to what we had envisioned. Our crew maintained its consistency but did not add much to the excellence it had reached last season. In her book *The Color Purple*, Alice Walker wrote, "Time moves slowly, but passes quickly." Such was the fate of that year. Before long it was summer once more.

That summer the GW crew traveled with the Georgetown crew to Japan, on a trip paid for by various sponsors arranged through some Japanese universities. Standing out in America as a black man rowing in a predominately white sport is one thing, but imagine how estranged I felt in Japan, where I was one of the only black people anywhere. More than once I was mistaken for Magic Johnson. Apparently the basketball star was on a trip to the country at the same time, and as one of only a few black people around, the resemblance was an easy mistake for them to have made. Observing a new culture as an outsider made me realize how important it is to be tolerant of people and their ways, even when those people and habits are vastly different than one's own. There were many ways the cultural relativism struck me, and I savored the opportunity to learn about people and customs that were foreign to me.

We stayed in Toda City at the Mitsubishi Boat Club. Coincidentally, Tony Johnson had rowed in the 1964 Olympics held in Toda City. The experience was interesting on all aspects. We took off our shoes for every different occasion. There were bathroom slippers, dishwashing slippers, house slippers. Every moment provided new insights into another culture's way of life. One day we went to a lecture at a large auditorium at the University of Tokyo. Many of the students and professors were in attendance. As a member of the American delegation, I had been asked to give a speech about the job opportunities for college graduates in America. For the start of the speech I memorized a paragraph in Japanese. When I began speaking and did not stop using the Japanese language for a few minutes, the audience grew baffled. The translator stood silently and watched with a peculiar twist to his brow. The audience started to whisper. Then I reverted to English and a huge sigh passed through the room. The translator began working and the audience found it very amusing. By the end of my speech a number of students stood up and asked questions. Women asked questions like, "Do you feel that Japanese women should be given a chance to work outside of the house and take on more responsibility in the workforce?" Then a man would ask, "Would you agree that the place for women is in the home and they should not try to move beyond their domestic duties?" I was thrown in the midst of a controversial argument and both perspectives looked to me for an answer. How to respond without offending my hosts eluded me. I waited for the dialogue to cool down before I said, "All people should be able to pursue a fulfilling life." This probably wasn't the answer they were hoping for, but it was the best I could think of at the time.

Other episodes on the trip to Japan were equally as interesting. Our crew visited the classroom of various junior high students, and with them we sang children's songs and helped them practice their English. Another day we visited the mayor of Toda City, and another time we saw the training center for some sumo wrestlers. Prior to the wrestlers we had been looking over the heads of everyone we saw. No matter what we did, it remained obvious that we were all Americans. I felt somewhat estranged being uniquely black among Americans who already stood out as atypical. At the same time it also comforted me to feel like my difference was not based on something so superficial as skin color, but on a distinction I could share with all my white teammates. After all, it made no matter that I was a black American and others were white Americans. We all stood out and had our own distinctively

American ways of operating. Feeling a part of that group — that melting pot of America group — gave me a sense of comfort that is hard to describe. The Japanese culture struck me as gentle and impressive.

Not all was perfect about the trip. The rowing in Japan never proved too extraordinary. We beat the Japanese boats with relative ease and defeated a Georgetown crew comprised of six members of Georgetown's Heavyweight Varsity boat, a member of their 2V, and Conal Groom, one of the strongest lightweights in the country. Beating Georgetown, even when they weren't at full strength, was pretty exciting for my crew. Mostly, the trip enabled us to experience something unique together as a team. The perspective we gained from the cultural immersion made it worthwhile to have gone. By the time it ended, we were all aggravated with one another from sharing living quarters that were much smaller than what we were used to back home. Nevertheless, the trip had been a great success.

Back in the United States, the remaining days of summer passed by on the water, where I continued to train as a sculler. I was lucky enough to row with some of the country's top scullers: Greg Walker and Greg Mhyr. Greg Walker was a many time National Team member and Greg Mhyr was the only guy I know who could drink a six pack of beer and then go out and win a race. Soon my fourth year at GW began, but the collegiate season didn't appeal to me as much as it had in the past. The team had nominated me as their captain, but I declined the nomination. Although they wanted to place me in the leadership role officially, I did not want the position and the responsibility it entailed. Being a natural leader without the title of "captain" made more sense to me then, but from hindsight I can see that my decision was based more upon my disbelief that I deserved the position. The moment someone had the name "captain," he was expected to uphold a certain standard of leadership and moral navigation. That expectation turned me away. I much rather preferred the idea of leading by silent example. Besides, my interest in collegiate crew was waning, not so much because I didn't love rowing, but because I loved being a senior in college more. It seemed like some of the other seniors were losing interest as well. Being a captain with such indifference would not have been good for me or for the team. When I looked around at the other athletes, there just wasn't the passion of years before. We had the talent, we had the experience, but I sensed less enthusiasm and intensity.

Yes, I still loved rowing, and yes, I considered myself the best rower on the team. But going out at night, playing my saxophone and enjoying the thrills of a normal college student just seemed more appealing than hitting the water with the first break of dawn. My silent leadership strategy didn't set a good example, at least not to the younger rowers. With the talent I had, and the commitment I had given in years past, I should have been that "love to row guy" everyone hated off the water but loved to have in the boat. But I was tired of it. Rowing still mattered to me, but I didn't have the same zip in my step when walking down to the boathouse. Throughout the season I nevertheless trained hard and gave my best when I was on the water. To have done anything less would have been a discredit to myself and an injustice to the members of my crew. The cycle of my commitment had no method to explain it, other than weak versions of "senioritis" and burnout.

My sights were on the Olympic Sports Festival that would take place in Boulder, Colorado the summer after my senior year. In addition to the sweep rowing that I did for the team, I also kept training as a sculler in the single. Although I gave my all during the collegiate season, mentally I began to make the transition to being a post-college rower. For all my loss of enthusiasm, rowing was too meaningful to leave it for good. My time at GW had helped me in so many ways. Ultimately, it brought me from a young boy who had rowed for one year of high school to a young man prepared to continue with the sport well into the future. Naturally, the better I had become the more fun I had. GW had given me numerous memorable experiences, but I was starting to see that collegiate rowing was only just the beginning.

CHAPTER 3

The Catch

Why did I continue to row after college? In retrospect the answer comes easily. All the adventure, exhilaration, good laughs and diverse experiences that rowing had poured into my life gave me ample reasons to continue. My experiences with a boat had taken me all over the world. They had introduced me to people I never imagined I would have the opportunity to meet. The sport has enriched and textured my life with blessings that most people do not have the good fortune to have had. Thanks to the connections and journeys I have made through the sport, I now have a much broader view of the world. I can visit any number of foreign countries and have someone to look after me, and I have improved my general knowledge of the world around me. Certainly these are reasons to continue rowing, but they are only ancillary to my primary motivation in the sport. They are the cherry on top.

The real reason I row is fundamental: it makes me a better human being. Well sure, one may say, but what does *that* mean? There are many qualities that may make someone a good person. Someone may be courageous, or charming, intelligent, or generous. Listing adjectives could go on forever. Being "a better human being" is a vague and broad notion, open to many interpretations, none of them objective. When I say rowing makes me a better person, I refer specifically to a sense that rowing forces me to be more honest with myself. To succeed in rowing, and particularly in the single scull, I have had to examine myself thoroughly. What am I willing to commit? How far can my talent take me if I work hard? What do I really want? If I aspire to have what I really want, then the answers to these questions must be honest. The introspection must be sincere and the effort that follows must be steadfast. If I want to be the best, but I am not willing to commit myself, then I will never achieve what I want. Rowing thus demands not only honesty about myself, but also the implementation and execution of whatever means are necessary to reach my goals. These strike me as important qualities. Am I *really* willing to commit to the task of making the U.S. National Rowing Team? How honest with myself am I being?

I believe that all our actions in life, all our interests and pursuits, should be guided by thoughtful introspection and self-honesty. The path to becoming a better person can lead through many territories. It makes little difference what that territory happens to be, provided it fosters a personal growth that ultimately improves the world around us. Being honest with ourselves about who we are, what we want, and what we are prepared to do to accomplish it, seems like the only sure-fire path toward personal growth. Rowing draws that introspection and growth from me. After looking inside myself to make an honest assessment, it becomes much easier to engage the world around me with more compassion. The hang-ups I may have had before getting down to the essentials of Aquil Abdullah no longer disturb me. I realize the way I need to live my life, and I try my hardest to live that way. Rowing has taught me the value of friendship, dependability, hard work, thoughtfulness, and, when necessary, being a tough guy. It is nice to have a better sense of what I value most. There is no doubt in my mind that rowing has brought about that realization. Now my task remains to sustain self-honesty and to utilize my answers in ways that will help me achieve my goals.

All this is easy to say now, from a more experienced perspective with a few years behind me. But this clarity wasn't always the case. After finishing my eligibility at George Washington University, I had to decide how serious I wanted to become about the sport. The decision to continue rowing had already been made, but did I just want to do it because it was fun? Was my only goal to make the Olympic Sports Festival in Boulder, Colorado? No and no. Going to the festival would be fun, but it would prove less difficult than anticipated. What I really wanted was something more. I wanted a spot on the U.S. National Sculling Team in the upcoming Atlanta Olympics.

During the summer of 1995 I competed in the U.S. Nationals and earned an invitation to the Olympic Sports Festival in Boulder. The competition at Nationals was strong, but I managed to make the Festival as I had hoped. A developmental group of sixteen scullers were selected. We trained in Augusta, Georgia for a short time before heading across the country to Colorado. Although the Festival was important for crew, my invitation to participate did not mean I would be an Olympian. For other sports like track and field, the Olympic Sports Festival played a more significant role. Some great athletes were there. In rowing, our group of sixteen made four quadruple sculls, representing the northern, southern, eastern and western parts of the United States. When I arrived, I was thrilled about competing in a large athletic festival with so many high caliber athletes. If at that point there were still any lingering doubts about whether to continue rowing, they were dispelled shortly. My boat finished in second place, and my incentive to continue shot through the roof. Unlike in college, now my motivation was much more than doing well at intercollegiate regattas. The Dad Vail Championships were nothing compared to the Olympics. The Festival gave me a taste of what the Olympics were all about. It was a small taste, but enough to stoke my fire.

When the Festival in Boulder finished, I returned home to Washington, DC, and lived at home with my mother. Before graduating from George Washington I still had some classes to finish, so I spent some time in school. Meanwhile I trained at Potomac Boat Club and took a job with Photon Research Associates. Between my new job as a computer systems administrator, finishing my class work and training, the summer flew to an end. That fall the big races would begin.

My first Speed Order race had 36 competitors. All I hoped was to make the cut of the top 18. It turned out I finished with one of the best times of all those competing. There were no slouches out there, either. Cyrus Beasley raced, as did Brian Jamison, Eric Mueller, David Gleason, Brad Layton and Jason Gails. Many of these guys would compete for seats in the quad for the 1996 Olympics. To finish among the best as a youngster fresh out of college was a big deal for me. These were the guys I watched race in the Nationals in years before. To me they belonged on a pedestal; they were the best single scullers in the country. Then when I held my own it occurred to me that I was up there among their ranks. The performance meant a lot to me, but others were not yet convinced.

Igor Grinko, then the coach of the U.S. National Team, applauded my results but otherwise brushed me aside and told me to keep on training. He invited some other rowers to train in Augusta with the U.S. Team that would try to make the Olympics. One could understand that he wasn't looking to develop any young oarsmen with the Olympics looming so close at hand. But his hesitance to invite me while at the same time inviting others whose performance had not been as strong as mine was something that would happen more than once.

At the start of 1996, at the next Speed Order race in Augusta, Georgia, I rowed the single again. Again I made the final and finished in the top tier. Also again, Igor overlooked my accomplishments. He invited several others to train at the High Altitude Camp in Colorado Springs, Colorado. For whatever his reasons, he had invited to Colorado Springs at least seven other single scullers who I had defeated on the water. Was I being subjected to some racial prejudice because he had something against people of black skin? I don't believe so. Was he opposed to my lack of height or weight compared with some other rowers? Perhaps. What it most likely came down to was Igor didn't believe I could move boats. He saw that my ergometer scores were lower than others and figured I could not move team boats the way others could. Although I believed I had proven him false by performing well on the water (and I had the racing times to prove it), he saw otherwise. It is a shame I was not given more favor for my performances. I wasn't after anything more than anyone else. All I wanted was the same opportunity that he had chosen to give to others. When this didn't happen, I took my training elsewhere.

That winter a bunch of guys went to Tampa, Florida to train to make the double boat that would row in the Olympic Trials later that year. John Righini was rowing with Steve Tucker, and I went along with them. We lived cramped in a one-bedroom motel room with a mini-fridge and microwave. The living was hard and frugal. We became experts in the art of peanut butter and jelly sandwiches, and I made a masterful microwave omelet. Notwithstanding the living situation, being down south in the winter was a great decision. We didn't have to crack away the ice from the water to lay our boats down like we would have up north. At nights Tampa offered a variety of places for me to bring my saxophone and have a jam session with other bands.

I rowed in the doubles camp and didn't do very well. No matter what boat they put me in, I was the anchor that slowed it down. Soon it occurred to me that the fastest boat from the camp would seat Dave

Lafevere and Scott Shore. It didn't take much to see I wasn't going to make a boat in the double for that year's Olympic Trials. At the time, Ted Nash, who coached at Pennsylvania Athletic Club and had accomplished a great deal in his own rowing career, was coaching Michelle Knox and Jennifer Devine to row in the double. In his deep booming voice Ted said to me, "Young man, if you want to train with us you're more than welcome." Since I had already realized I would not be in the top double coming out of the training group I had been with, I decided it would be a great opportunity to return to the single and train under Ted. Although I could move the single, when I had tried to row in some team boats my results were not as strong. Maybe Igor was right to doubt my ability. Practicing against Michelle and Jennifer under Ted's instruction would give me the chance to return my focus to the single, where I felt most comfortable.

I trained under Ted until his camp left Tampa in mid-winter, then I returned to Philadelphia for a few weeks to train under him up north. When my finances ran low I went back home to Washington to keep training and to save some money. All this time on the water had improved my speed a great deal. Springtime arrived and the ice melted from the river. I trained under Ken Dreyfuss at Potomac Boat Club. As my rowing career advanced, Ken would become a fixture of support through all my endeavors. He had coached at the U.S. Naval Academy and at Stanford University, and brought to my training an unconditional generosity of effort. Ken helped my form, and I continued to pick up speed, but I was still relatively new to the single. I didn't know where I stood compared with the other single scullers who would compete in the Olympic Trials. Ken assured me that I could only control what I was doing and that I need not focus on anyone else. Besides, I would learn about the others soon enough. Time for the Trials was upon us.

We loaded up the trailer from Potomac Boat Club and headed down to Gainsville, Georgia for the 1996 U.S. Olympic Trials. When we arrived, a big hubbub was made about me being one of only two African-Americans competing in the regatta. I tried to focus on the racing. It would be a big challenge. People insisted that my skin color was of great importance, but I did my best to dismiss those notions and concentrate on the task ahead. Most competitors in my first race were people I had not raced before. James Martinez was among them. He had been the lightweight single sculler for the U.S. National Team in previous years. For the Olympics there is no category for the lightweight single, so James would have to compete against heavyweight scullers like Cyrus Beasley and John Riley. Cyrus had been the National Team's heavyweight single sculler for the past few years, and John had filled the role for a few years before that. Everyone anticipated the match-up. All I hoped to do was give a strong performance that would not disappoint me. No one expected me to do well. There was no reason anyone should have.

I always try to enter an event with the attitude that every race is the most important race of my life, but at this point there really had been no other race of equal significance. Because it was an Olympic year, they used new technology that I had not used before. Instead of allowing a boat's bow to float along the water and be held by a stake boat person before the race begins, at the Trials they used a lock-in system that held the boat in place with mechanical clamps. Out on the water, clamped in place, I thought that winning my heat was well within reach. Of the competition around me, James Martinez would make the toughest challenge, but I thought I could beat him if I could temper his quick start.

With the starting signal our clamps unlocked; the race started as planned. James and I vied for top position. After 500 meters he went out to a lead, and sustained it at 1000. By that point both he and I were out on the crowd. *Do I push it or rest?* I pondered the best strategy. Rather than try to catch him, I decided the best choice would be to conserve my energy for the repecharge later that day.

The repecharge is a second chance race for those who don't win their heat. Without it the sport would not be the same, since conditions and unforeseeable circumstances can easily alter the expected outcomes of any event. This way the best oarsmen are more likely to proceed to the finals. Finishing second in my heat gave me the top seed in my repecharge, meaning I had to compete only against those who had come in no higher than third in their heats. With the higher seed and my energy saved since that morning, I won the repecharge without drama. The victory placed me in the semi-finals against competition that continued to strengthen. After racing, my coach Ken Dreyfuss came to give me his support. We talked about a strategy for the semi-final, and he prepared me for an even tougher challenge than what I had already faced.

The semi-final held a lot more excitement. Three semi-finals were conducted. The top two finishers from each semi-final would advance to the final race to see who would represent the United States in the

1996 Olympics. My luck positioned Cyrus Beasley in my semi-final. His strength and speed far surpassed my own, so the race was really for second place. Pete Michaud and I were the top contenders following Cyrus. Pete and I had started out sculling together at Potomac Boat Club. Like me, Pete was a football player turned rower, and more so than me, he was a physically menacing character. We exchanged strokes and stayed even throughout the course. He pulled. I pulled. We were synchronized. Both matched the other in exertion and strength. Toward the end, the cheering fans let us know the finish line was closer and closer. I made my surge. *Pull. Pull.* Pete matched my strokes. My only chance was to get more drive from each stroke than he could. *Pull.* I pressed ahead to a small lead. With only a second between us, my bow was first to cross the line. So spent was my energy that I blacked out from sheer exhaustion. It was okay, though, because I'd bought some time. Yes, I was exhausted, but I had also made tomorrow's finals.

Meanwhile John Riley, who, on the other side of the bracket, was likely to be Cyrus's strongest competition, had the worst possible luck. On the day of the race he was in a car accident and suffered injuries forcing him to withdraw from the regatta. A cloud of disappointment and sorrow filled the atmosphere. People were beginning to wonder about the chances of this new young rower named Aquil Abdullah. I had not expected to make the finals, and being there pitted me against big names like Cyrus, James Martinez, Pat Sweeny and Matt Madagan. Each was known as one of the country's best in the event. Then there I was, at six feet two inches, one hundred and seventy three pounds. With the exception of James, I was one of the smallest competitors in my event.

It may seem odd, but I never felt small. Even the next afternoon, in the finals race that could qualify me for the Olympic Team, when I lined up at the starting point across from much larger and more experienced oarsmen, I was more excited than intimidated. At that point in my rowing career I had not competed in a more important or more electrifying event. In the semi-final I had raced so hard to defeat Pete Michaud that I didn't have much energy left. Despite the confidence and exhilaration I carried over to the finals, my results on the last day were not as wonderful as they had been before.

The first race unfolded with a surprising start. Pat Sweeny pushed out to the lead over Cyrus. I managed to stay even with James Martinez. Matt Madagan was in back and I liked my chances. Then

Cyrus made a move on Pat. His power was too great. After Cyrus made his move, James made a gradual drive ahead of me. Matt Madagan crept in. The others were moving out. *Beat out Matt, Aquil. Come on.* Matt and I battled for fourth. As we neared the finish line, James continued with his steady advance and moved ahead of Pat. The order was Cyrus, James, Pat, me then Matt. After the quick start, Pat could not sustain so intense a pace. I saw him slowing down and told myself, *I can catch him.* Drawing my stroke rate up, pulling my oars' broadside through the water's resistance, I increased the lead on Matt. With 500 meters to go I was alone in fourth and still eyeing Pat Sweeny to take third. Coming in to the grandstand section of the course, the crowd's cheers brought us toward the finish. I looked over and saw Pat to my side. *I can still catch him. I'm right there.* The crowd's enthusiasm surged my adrenaline. With all I had, I pulled. I kicked my knees down and pressed my feet into the foot stretcher stroke by stroke. *Almost there. Close. A little harder.* It was no use. The race was too near its end. While I held off Matt to finish fourth, I could not catch Pat or the others.

Never did I stand much of a chance to finish first, but I had rowed a strong race and felt good about my performance. With a three-race format, my chances to be that year's Olympic single sculler were still alive. The winner must win two of the three races. It was possible, but I was cooked with exhaustion. In the second final I finished fourth again, with the disappointment of a poor performance. These Trials had sapped every last bit of energy I had. My results in the second final were the same as the first, without the personal satisfaction of at least having challenged others for a higher finish. I would not be the Olympic single sculler in 1996. Still I thought that a fourth place spot in the single sculls at the U.S. Olympic Trials might earn me an invitation to train with the Olympic Team as a spare. If a quad and double boat still needed filling, that left six places for talented scullers like myself. Top four or not, Igor still wasn't convinced that I had the necessary skills. Coach Grinko gave me some encouragement but told me to try again next time. His words crashed atop me and left a ruinous disappointment. All I could do was take some private consolation in my performance. Even though I had not made the team, the 1996 Olympic Trials had given me the confidence of knowing that in four years the story would be different. Then I would be bigger, stronger and faster.

That summer I went back to Washington, DC and trained on the Potomac with Mike Porterfield. Mike was there training for the World Championship Trials for non-Olympic boats. In addition to rowing on several national teams, and in the double sculls at the Olympic Trials, Mike had been a member of the sweeping four without coxswain that won the silver medal at the 1993 World Championships. One of Mike's greatest gifts is the enthusiasm he brings to every task. We worked hard together, on the water and off. Sometimes we carried 25-pound weights in each hand while doing lunges down K Street near Potomac Boat Club. Other times we rowed at race speed down the Potomac in mid-summer humidity. My chance at the Olympics had died, but I still wanted to improve. Mike planned to row the sweep boat of four with coxswain in the 1996 World Championship Trials. I set my sights on single sculling at the U.S. National Championships.

For a while, Mike went to train in San Diego, but he returned to Washington before the National Championships, which were coming up in Indianapolis, Indiana. Despite the title, the National Championships weren't all that they claimed. The best oarsmen in the country sometimes skipped the National Championships, so the championship race did not really indicate the nation's best oarsman. For instance, all three scullers who defeated me in the Olympic Trials would be absent at the 1996 Nationals. Cyrus was training for the Olympics. Pat Sweeny had retired. James Martinez, the lightweight single sculler, went to train for the World Championships where he could compete in the lightweight single event that the Olympics excluded. I entered the National Championships with the top seed.

Eagle Creek in Indianapolis can be very windy. Some rowers know the location as Windyanapolis or Windy Indy. When the water is calm the course is beautiful. As far as I ever saw, it just wasn't calm with any consistency. I had rowed Eagle Creek a few times before, and had watched several races on the course as well. The conditions worried me, but I knew what to expect. Without the same caliber of competition as I had faced at the Olympic Trials, the first few races went as expected. I advanced to the final without many obstacles.

As luck would have it, my birthday fell in the middle of the races. I had been racing in a Potomac Boat Club tank top and a pair of rowing shorts that had holes through the seams. Ken Dreyfuss saw me after a practice race and took me over to a Regatta Sports Rowing Apparel tent, where he bought me a pair of rowing shorts. "Happy Birthday," he said. Ken was the king of the kind gesture, the saint of generosity. With my new shorts, I now had the look of a champion, but looking good and winning the finals were two different things. A tough challenge remained.

In the final I faced Andy McMarlin and Will Fisher. Andy McMarlin and an oarsman named Ty Benion had won in the double at the Olympic Trials, but because the U.S. double did not qualify for the Olympics at the World Championships in 1995, their double had to travel to Lucerne after the Olympic Trials to earn their Olympic bid. In Lucerne the double did not qualify, so Andy came back and decided to row the single in the National Championships. Will Fisher was considered one of the country's top single scullers, and he had beaten me on many previous occasions. That year he had rowed in a quad that did not qualify for the Olympics, so he was back in the single at Nationals.

The race went off with the expected winds whipping over the water. Careful not to lose my balance, I took a small lead. There were others in the field, but only Will and Andy stayed close. For 1500 meters I sustained the advantage. They neither gained nor fell behind. By then the wind became a non-factor. We were coming toward the finish. *Okay, Aquil. Get it done.* With slightly over 500 meters remaining, I made my move. Andy still stayed with me. At that point in the course a marina with sailboats comes into view. This area had been my marker indicating where I should press for the final sprint to the finish. Strategically, I have always thought it best advised to make my final surge before my opponent makes his. In the single in particular, if I can make my opponent give up and think he has no chance to catch me, then my work is already accomplished. The task can be difficult if not downright impossible when facing oarsmen who are mentally Herculean. At this level, my opponents had the confidence that they could come back even when they were down. Trying nevertheless to pull ahead with about a quarter of the race remaining, I increased the stroke rate. *Pull Aquil. Pull.* Andy stayed with me. The fans' screams rang across the water. At 250 meters to go the buoys turned orange and I nodded my head. *Last thirty strokes.* After that I bore down and pulled the oars through the water with every last fragment of determination and strength that I possessed. *A little bit more*, I kept telling myself. *Just a little bit more. Harder. Pull harder.* My boat began to surge ahead. I crossed the finish line a national champion.

The first person to greet me when I came off the water was Mike Porterfield. I was exhausted but he picked me up with a great bear hug and tossed me in the air. "Well done," he cheered. "Well done!" Other fans and supporters began to come down and give their congratulations. Although the country's top oarsmen were not all present, and although I had been favored to win, the victory was important. I knew if I could continue to improve, then I would someday be on the line wearing the red, white and blue. It was meaningful for me that I was expected to have won and I still lived up to the expectations. After I took my bearings on shore, word started to spread that I might be the first African-American to win a U.S. National Championship. Officials went back to the regatta history and verified previous results. Their suspicions were correct. In 1996 my win was the first of its kind for an African-American.

Following that victory people have asked me what it feels like to have done something that no one in my race had ever done before. African-Americans have approached me proudly and praised me for all that I've done for my people. As flattered as I am by what I have accomplished, I hesitate to tout it as something larger than what it was. Part of me felt like I truly had broken a barrier for African-Americans in the sport of rowing, and perhaps in society as a whole. Civil rights had come a long way in the last century, but while the playing fields had leveled a little between the races, the fight against prejudice and injustice was far from over. If my victory represented a victory in this fight, then I am glad to have done so. Most of all, I am just glad to be another rower who, on that particular day, had what it took to be the best.

The National Championships were my last significant race of the summer. I took a short break after the regatta in Indianapolis, then returned to Washington to become a full-time employee at Photon Research Associates. For a short time I stayed at home with my mother, but then I moved in with Mike Porterfield, John Vaughan and Dan Allen. John had been a friend of Mike's dating back to high school and Dan coached at Georgetown. We got along well, and I spent the fall training for the Head races that would take place in Philadelphia and Boston. Having done well that summer, my enthusiasm for the sport shot to an all time high.

When Mike Porterfield went to coach at Potomac Boat Club with Ken Dreyfuss, who had been coaching me up until then, my relationship with Mike became more stressed than it had been before. Living together with a coach poses a number of problems. For one, it is difficult to function socially with someone who holds over you a position of authority. Second, Mike demanded a lot of me as a rower. When I was unable to meet his demands, tension mounted between us. At that stage I was probably not Mike's star pupil. I had a lot of maturing to do before my potential could be maximized with hard and persistent work. Having competed himself, Mike knew what it took to reach the top as an oarsman. All he wanted was that I train rigorously enough to reach that echelon. Although I also wanted to arrive at that level, my training still lingered a notch or two below what was needed to get there.

That fall I went to a Speed Order race and recorded a respectable time. Igor had asked a number of oarsmen to train down in Augusta, and finally, I was included. The invitation was nothing particularly special; it did not mean I had made, or even that I would make, the 1997 U.S. National Team. All it would do would give me a chance to train down south with very competitive rowers and to train within Igor's system. He told me I could do whatever I chose. Because I already had a job in Washington, and since I was happy with my living situation, I chose to stay in Washington where I trained hard for the remainder of the autumn. Turning down Igor after being so frustrated that he had neglected me before was not as big a decision as it may seem. Training with Igor in that instance would have conferred no special honor to me. Besides, I already had a good system worked out in Washington.

After a fall of training on the Potomac, the winter arrived sooner than expected. With December came another Speed Order in Augusta. Augusta that week was unusually cold. The heats were determined by ergometer tests inside where it was warm. Chronically poor on the erg, I clocked a time that placed me in one of the weaker heats. During my actual heat race, though, I moved the boat over the water much faster than my erg score would indicate. I won the heat and eventually advanced to the final. People started to turn their heads at my name. All by myself I'd earned a new respect in the sculling circuit. Because I'd gone about it on my own, and because I was still relatively new to it, I was still in awe of my competitors on the National Team.

In the Speed Order finals I felt strong and confident, even if I was awestruck by the caliber of my opponents. It was a cold morning over the water as we waited at the starting line. A faint fog flitted skyward from the surface. At that point in my career I had a slower start than

I do now. When the race began, I pierced the fog in the middle of the pack. During my training that fall, I had worked on making solid and well timed moves. A move is basically a ten or twenty-stroke spurt when the oarsmen says, "Okay, for this spurt I'm going to buckle down and move the boat." My race strategy was to make three moves, the first at 500 meters into the race, then another at 1000 meters, and a third at 1350, just before the final stretch for the finish. This third move had the most strategy behind it, as most rowers don't make their third move until 500 meters remain in the course. I always thought, it's better to put the pressure on my opponent before he has the chance to put it on me. Just when the others slowed down from their second surge — usually ten or fifteen strokes beyond the 1500 meter mark — I would make a final push for the finish. That final stretch would always be an all out effort. Provided I had the stamina, why not make that final surge a bit early and try to force my opponent to give up? In the final race I stuck to my plan. My surges came at the right times, but they were not backed by enough power. Although I did not win, I finished in the top portion of the group.

After my performance, this time I was asked by Igor to train at the High Altitude Camp at the Olympic Training Center in Colorado Springs. This was the chance I'd been waiting for. There was honor involved in this invitation, not just a half-hearted offer to move down to Augusta. Finally it seemed like I had earned some respect as a single sculler. For the first time I could be training among America's top rowers. It was an offer I would not refuse. Although a part of me still revered and stared with amazement at the rowers who would soon be my partners, I felt prepared to move up to their level — as much as that was possible.

Physiologically speaking, I am not one of the most gifted athletes in the rowing world. Nor do I have particularly good size. I am not the smallest or weakest oarsman, but I am weaker and shorter than most others in the elite circuit. This was especially true among my training partners in Colorado Springs. My deficiencies stood out more clearly when I performed the physiological fitness tests conducted by scientific experts in health and physical fitness at the Olympic Training Center.

Austere scientists milled about the laboratory in white coats, jotting notes on clipboards held close to their sides. All the athletes at the training center performed fitness tests for the scientists, rigged with the latest equipment in medical technology. As rowers, we were seated on ergs and fixed with sensors on different parts of our bodies. A contraption was also placed over each person's head, and our noses were shut off so we could only breathe from the mouth and into a tube that recorded our oxygen consumption. After I had been suited with the testing equipment, I started to row. Breathing from only the mouth made for a cotton-mouthed sensation that left me gagging and trying hard not to vomit. With about 500 meters left in the full 2000 meter ergometer test, my lungs burned like a torch lit inside my chest. At high altitude my time was not as good as the already mediocre erg times I recorded at sea level. The torch in my lungs did not relent, and all I wanted was to finish. When I did finish, a man in a white coat came immediately and pricked me to test my blood's lactic acid level. Then the coated men pushed me ahead to the sub-max testing, where I had to row some more at various splits of intensity. Again they pricked me to test my lactic acid level. I rowed until I could no longer hold the split and they took some more measurements using the contraption on my head. Finally, the people in lab coats placed reflective dots over my body on the major joints: elbows, knees, shoulders, wrists, ankles and hips. Using these reflectors the scientists connected the dots and created a computerized version of my stroke's biomechanics.

All these tests fascinated me and made my experience at the Olympic Training Center more exciting. It was somewhat despairing, however, to find that all my training mates were more physically gifted. For instance, some rowers had VO2 maximums at 6.8 liters per minute. My maximal oxygen uptake was only 5.6. It bothered me at first, knowing I was inferior. Then I realized that I wouldn't have been there if I didn't deserve it. Besides, wasn't a camp meant to facilitate one's improvement?

High Altitude Camp did plenty to improve me, and even more to exhaust me. Our schedule was rigorous. It wasn't long before we started calling it "pain camp" because we were so sore from the intensity of our training. Let alone the difficulty of rowing at high altitude, our daily schedule was bad enough. The day began with three hours of weight training in the morning. Igor's weight training program differed from any I had ever tried. Just to keep up with the other rowers I felt that I had to work twice as hard and lift weights beyond my normal capability. When the first weight training portion of the day ended, we took a brief break, then hit the gym again a little later, often to lift more weights. Putting my body under this sudden burst of heavy lifting had the imaginable effect of making my joints and muscles incredibly sore. By the second day I was in utter agony. No pharmacy full of painkillers or muscle treatments could have alleviated the pain I felt. In the evenings we went for a swim or did some other sort of aerobic work, but that did little to ease my pain. All I could do was grit my teeth and try to get through the next exercise.

As difficult as it was, the bulk of our schedule excluded rowing. We managed to fit in a lot of time on the erg, and we did so much running we might have been training with the U.S. track team. As wondrous as I had imagined High Altitude Camp beforehand, once I arrived I soon learned all there was to it: working out, eating and sleeping. Not much else fit in the schedule. On our "off day" we climbed Pike's Peak — a work out all its own — and by the time the week and a half was over, I was exhausted. The entirety of my physical energy had depleted, which explains why it was a miracle when I left the camp invigorated in spirit.

When I returned to Washington to train, my recorded times on the water had improved. How I have succeeded in moving a boat against athletes whose physical fitness capacity exceeds my own has been a wonder of mine for many years. Maybe it's another miracle. My competitors do not just *seem* bigger, stronger and more full of breath. They have been scientifically *proven* to have these advantages. If there were an explanation I might offer, it would have to be the intangible "feeling" I have for driving a boat across the water. My rowing technique is far from perfect, but I have always felt a sense for how to bring speed to the boat's movement.

After some time in Washington, where I combined my feeling for movement with a greater effort to hone the technical aspects of my stroke, I went to the Speed Order that preceded the National Single's Trials. The Speed Order did not mean much. It helped people gauge where everyone stood before the Trials. I wanted an idea of who was the best, and what it took to get there. When Jamie Koven raced the single and won with little difficulty, I saw which direction to follow. Nobody was a faster single sculler than Jamie. I asked if I could spend some time training with him. He was going to train in Princeton at the time, and he said if I cleared it with Coach Mike Teti, training with him would be fine.

Coach Teti gave his approval and I spent a little over a week training with Jamie in Princeton. Although I thought I was starting to become a more talented rower, Jamie showed me quickly how vast the difference was between the top and myself. Just to stay with him in a twenty stroke piece I had to start an entire length ahead, and even in minor skills like the ability to steer a boat straight, I was far below the talents of Jamie and the other oarsmen on the water. Coach Teti hollered at me for rowing in front of Jamie and subjecting him to my wake, impeding his progress. At one point he threatened that if I interfered with Jamie again I would never again be allowed to row in Princeton. Somehow my steering improved by magnitudes.

When the National Single's Trials arrived I was ready to prove my skills. I already knew that Jamie's times were impressive. Cyrus Beasley rowed in the Single's Trials that year, too, and he was also fast. Training in Princeton had given me some perspective on where I stood, and as that perspective had taught me, I was not at the top. My performance in the Trials remained consistent with my speculation that my skills were not sufficient to have much to prove. I advanced to the first final but did not make the cut for the second final in the best out of three progressions. Meanwhile, Jamie had won in the first final, not to my surprise. Cyrus was his closest challenger. To force a third race, Cyrus had to win on the second day. As I watched from the sidelines, he went out with an explosion. I couldn't see how anyone could beat Jamie, but Cyrus gave a great start. By the end his bursts of exertion were too exhausting. Steady-mannered Jamie passed by for the win. The 1997 Single's Trials showed no surprises, though they provided some great excitement. My results were no surprise either, but there remained in me the sour aftertaste of not doing as well as I thought I could.

After the Trials, I imagined that a fourth place finish in my second year there would earn me a spot on the team of seven scullers that would represent America in the World Championships. It was not that easy. Igor had already selected the quad to consist of Brian Jamison, Chris Duffy, Brad Layton and Cyrus Beasley. There was a quad camp, but it was mere formality. Anyone with straw in his noggin could see that the quad was already selected. Without dispute, the athletes in the 1997 World Championship quad were top-notch oarsman; but, it frustrated me to know in advance that, even though Igor invited me to train in Augusta, I still wouldn't be in the quad. Since Jamie had won the Single's Trial, he would row the single, leaving open only two more sculling seats on the National Team. Those seats were in the double, and I shifted my focus to earning a spot in that boat.

To train for the double I remained in Augusta under Igor's coaching. As I had experienced at High Altitude Camp, Igor's method for training athletes was grueling, as if intended to build athletes capable of running through brick walls. I thought High Altitude Camp was tough, but the intensity didn't wane in Augusta. Never in my life, even to this day, have I trained more than I did while in Augusta rowing under Igor. Igor believed in his system, and the silver medal that he produced in the quadruple scull in the Atlanta Games gave a strong indication of his method's solidity. When I trained in Igor's system I believed in his system as any good student believes in his teacher. I hoped that after working under his program I might earn a place on the 1997 National Sculling Team. If anything, working under Igor would be a good way to ensure that I trained myself to be the type of rower he sought when selecting oarsmen for the National Team's double and quad. The problem was, the quad was already selected, and no matter how hard I worked, I could not shake the impression that my teacher did not share an equal amount of faith in me as his pupil.

The remaining scullers rowed in a double's matrix where each oarsman rowed with each of the others until the fastest combination could be found. After I won all of my seat races, Igor placed me in a double with Eric Eldridge. At the time, our boat was probably the fastest combination in Augusta, excluding those in the quad. Unfortunately, as the summer moved on Eric and I only became slower. We finished fourth at the Double's Trials for the double scull.

With the quad boat already determined, and with Andy McMarlin and Steve George placed in the double after winning the Double's Trials, there were no places left for me on the team. I talked to Igor about my options and he suggested I remain in Augusta, as there was a chance I could be a spare. After continuing to train there, sure enough, he named me as a spare on the team that would soon compete in the World Championships in France. Although the honor gave little consolation when my real goal was to be a true representative, it was an opportunity I could not refuse.

The time of my involvement on the U.S. National Team rings with memories of the sort best crystallized to music. It was a special time, filled with stories and laughs that words are inadequate to describe. The spares for National Teams have unique responsibilities. In part they are there to be prepared in the event that other oarsmen are injured. Another part is to go out and have some fun so those who are actually competing can live vicariously through the spare's stories. I also had the third responsibility of participating in the opening ceremonies as the team's flag bearer. Each duty gave me some fond memories. Cyrus once burned his thumb and I replaced him for a time in the quad. The local pubs and casinos gave me ample time to fall in love with French women and goof around with my roommate Jason Read, who was a sweep spare. And bearing the flag at the opening parade allowed me to feel like an important part of the U.S. Team. All my memories are fond ones, whether bearing the flag or watching Jamie row to world championship victory in a single's race to match no other. More than any failure or personal accomplishment, when recalling the 1997 World Championships, my mind preserves the musical memories of being in France as part of a team of friends.

Though my memories would last forever, I was still not satisfied with the outcome of my performances. After the World Championships, it was back to the water. Next year would be the year, I told myself. There was always next year. But the time following the World Championships in 1997 was a troubling period for me. I had serious decisions to make about my involvement in the sport in the years ahead. Sure, some success had come my way, but not nearly the success for which I aspired. Was it time to give it up, or did I want to go on with the struggle?

To think about my future and have some fun while at it, I drove up the East Coast with one of my good friends, Chris Duffy. Along the way we stopped at his parents' house, where his father and he destroyed me in golf, and his mother couldn't feed me enough. Chris made his first National Team in 1997, and remained in the quad through 1999. In 2000, he was selected as the spare for the Olympic Sculling Team. At the time, Chris was heading to Nova Scotia to see his future wife. I had him drop me off in Boston, where I began to question whether I really wanted to continue rowing.

As I expected, Boston gave me just what I needed: a replenished soul. I stayed with a friend of mine named Alex Selvig, and his brother, Fabio, in their house in Brighton. Alex had extended a welcome invitation to stay there whenever I happened to pass through town, so I took him up on his offer. We had fun together, and I attempted half-heartedly to sort through the possible paths my future might take. Should I return to school? Should I go full force into a career? Should I continue to row? The fun was intense, but it did not last long. When I ran short of money, I figured it was time to go home. Alex drove me to the train station and I left Boston, headed for Washington. I still had no idea what to do once I arrived. As if by habit, in Washington I started training again. Not certain of where the months ahead would lead, I went to work for a temp agency to make some money and plant myself on the ground again. Although I trained, I had not fully committed myself enough to improve like I once wanted. What did I want? Before long I ran into Owen Lewis, my former boss at Photon Research Associates, and a member of Potomac Boat Club. He told me that I better stop filing papers and return instead to Photon Research Associates where I could do something useful. The offer was too good to decline, and once again I settled into living in Washington.

That October I moved back home with my mother. Mike Porterfield was again coaching at Potomac Boat Club with Ken Dreyfuss. As a good friend of mine, Mike could see that I was not committed to rowing the way he felt I should be committed. Mike constantly hounded me to work harder and to put in more time on the water. At first this pressure brought great stress to our relationship. Only later, with retrospect, have I realized that Mike encouraged me to work hard because he saw the potential within me. That potential would go to waste if not cultivated with dedication and hard practice.

The dedication just wasn't there. I didn't know how much longer I wanted to keep rowing. It had been nice as a spare at the 1997 World Championships, but even that was lackluster compared to the gold that I really wanted. Hadn't I worked hard enough? Didn't I deserve to have more success? It didn't much matter. Rowing became tiresome to me. My goals were still so far away and I didn't have the energy to pursue them the way I'd have to if they were going to be achieved.

That winter I pretty much disappeared from the boathouse. My doubts about rowing showed themselves in a general indifference toward the sport. It wasn't that I'd abandoned it, just that I was too uncertain about how to proceed. I had to distance myself from everyone else who approached the sport with nose down and course straight ahead. It would have been too difficult for me in that time to be around others who were more committed — others who had the commitment I knew was necessary if I truly wanted success. Likewise, I would have been a bad influence on those who had that commitment, so I just kept my distance. Instead I spent time lifting weights at the gym. Though my stroke didn't improve, I gained a much needed ten pounds of muscle.

In November, when the chance again came to attend High Altitude Camp, I was extended an invitation but decided not go. I'd determined to train my way or not at all. For a large portion of the winter I divided my time between the weight room and the water, but through it all, I was by myself. The solitude gave me a chance to figure some things out. I turned to my saxophone. Music was just what I needed. Playing an instrument released all the tension that only accumulated when I rowed and faced the pressure of living up to so much potential on the water. With music there was no sense of expectation. There were no coaches telling me I could be really good *if only* I would do this, or *if only* I would do that. All I had to do was pick up my sax and find the groove.

By January, my skills playing the saxophone earned me an invitation to play in a band that would tour with a popular group called G Love and Special Sauce. This opportunity was a musician's dream — hitting the road on a rock and roll tour. I couldn't fathom passing it up to stay and train. But I had come a long way in rowing, and despite my misgivings, I was equally as caught by the allure of continuing my personal training regimen. To my mother, the tour was just another unneeded distraction in my life. She raised her voice in protest. No matter how she objected, the tour was too compelling to resist. Besides, I thought, it would only last for a month. How unfit could I become?

How little I knew about life on the road with a rock band. After two weeks of dissipation, my body craved the release of exercise. We traveled in a plush bus and had a great time, but after the first few nights spent staying awake drinking until the crack of dawn, I knew it was too much for me. How could I let a whole month slide and hope to pick up rowing just a step behind where I left off? I was weary of rowing, but not ready to waste everything I'd worked so many years to achieve. Soon I started lifting weights at hotels, and running when I had the chance. My band's last concert was at a club called the 40 Watt, in Athens, GA, and some of my friends who were training in Augusta came up to see me. That was the moment when I realized how much I missed the sport. G Love and Special Sauce were headed to Japan, and Firstborn, the band I played with, was headed back to Augusta where I had first joined their ranks. Some rumors lingered about a record deal, which we all welcomed with fingers crossed, but the record company wanted to make some changes in the composition of the band, and the deal didn't go through. After just over a month on the road, I returned home to DC, still essentially at the start of the new year. Once again, I was eager to train hard.

Enthusiasm does not imply talent. My enthusiasm for rowing may have surged back to a high level, but how fast would I be on the water? Oddly, I had improved. When I went back to Potomac Boat Club I went out in an old rickety boat and took my warm up. The stroke felt strong and I was glad to be back in my element. Then when I rowed some pieces against other rowers, I was surprised at how convincingly I beat them. Nobody could understand it. "But he hasn't even been training," people would say. "It doesn't make sense." They were right. No sense of it could be made.

Resolving my mental uncertainty toward rowing seemed to have brought a physical result. I was still upset at how things had gone for me rowing-wise, but I'd worked too hard to quit. My outlook flipped back toward the world of crew, but this time I had a better perspective. I had the sense to appreciate a good balance. If I hadn't gone on the tour, it would not have taken much for me to burn out from rowing. With my musical break, I realized what mattered most. My mental and physical energy returned to where my heart needed to be: on the water.

No matter how to explain it, my speed improved. Now, rather than train only for the 1998 National Single's Trials as I had planned, I decided to compete in a Speed Order race to see how I compared with other oarsmen from outside the Washington area. When I finished in the top three at Speed Orders people started asking, "What kind of training program have you been on?" All I could do was shrug and smile. Never underestimate the importance of mental rejuvenation and clarity of purpose. Although I hadn't been training hard all year, I started to train once more. The National Single's Trials were around the corner.

The 1998 Trials in Augusta held one of the best races I have ever seen in the single sculling event. Unfortunately, I wasn't in it. I advanced into the first round of the finals, but from lack of training could not obtain the edge that might have thrust me higher than a fifth place finish and into the top tier of finalists. Instead I watched Jamie Koven and Don Smith race for the win. These two oarsmen gave anyone who watched a great example of how well tuned an excellent oarsman should look. In 1998 they were truly the best elite single scullers in the country. As I watched them race, something inside me felt wrong. I was tired of watching these finals. Like I felt in my experience at George Washington with the Dad Vail Championships, I didn't want to be watching any more finals from the shore. I wanted to participate in them. What would I need to do?

After the Trials I sat down and did some serious thinking. Igor had suggested that I train with Cyrus Beasley and try to earn a place on the team in the double with him. I'd met Cyrus in 1994 when I was training in DC. Ken Dreyfuss had taken a bunch of scullers over to Occoquan, Virginia to row against the National Team members who were training in Virginia. Back then Igor was based in Virginia. I remember seeing Cyrus put his boat in the water and take off. He nearly flipped three times as he pulled away from the dock. I was rowing in a double with Pete Michaud, and we were getting pulverized by a couple of lightweights. As we finished our 500 meter piece I saw the singles coming down the course, and there was Cyrus. I think Cyrus was pretty new to sculling at that point, and water sprayed everywhere after each of his strokes. "What a mess," I said to myself. Then I looked at the bend in the shaft of his oars, and I said, "Damn, he's strong!" Cyrus went on to become one of the top single scullers in the country. He would make the perfect partner in the double.

Taking Igor's advice, I spoke with Cyrus about training together. He sounded willing, but he lived in Boston and did not want to leave the area for Augusta. In Boston he had his job and a home, and in Augusta all he would have was rowing. As nice as Augusta was to train, the job opportunities and non-rowing benefits of the area could not compare to larger cities up north. I decided to go train with Cyrus in Boston.

Any number of factors could explain what happened next. Malcolm Gefter from Cambridge boathouse helped get Cyrus and me a boat, and he arranged for us to row from Cambridge boathouse on the Charles River. For all the advantages we had, Cyrus and I could not move over the water. We were both proficient single scullers, but placed together in the same shell, something went wrong. Our styles were too different to find that intangible chemistry that makes a boat fast. On most days no coaches were there to help us with our training, so rather than find a common ground between the differences in our styles, Cyrus and I kept tugging along in our own distinct directions. Meanwhile, down in Augusta other double boats were setting their goals to beat our boat. Cyrus and I were the favorites to win, and we had the attitude that if we could only merge our two styles then no one could catch us. Other boats had the goal in mind of knocking us from our imagined throne. When a month passed and we drove to Indianapolis for the Double's Trials, we never accomplished what we wanted. As expected, we made the finals, but once there we lost two consecutive races.

By the weekend of the Double's Trials the quad had been selected, and with our failed attempt in the double, I was once again without a place on the National Team. Being a spare again did not particularly interest me. It had been a good experience in 1997, but I was tired of being outside looking in. No longer was I content with any title other than one of the very best scullers in the country. As my results had indicated, I still needed some work. The time came again to do a sincere and thorough evaluation of where I would take my rowing career.

✿　　✿　　✿　　✿　　✿

After the World Trials in 1998, it became clear that rowing demanded I be honest with myself. If I were just going to take an occasional interest in the sport, straying from training whenever I felt like it, or hitting the highways for a month on musical tours, I would never reach the level I wanted. Going on tour and stumbling upon a certainty of purpose had made a big difference. A mental improvement made a physical result in my rowing speed, but I still knew no mental adjustment would suffice if not coupled with a greater commitment to training. There was no sense pretending I had given all I had to give. I had not prepared myself as best as possible in my attempt to become a champion. If I wanted to be one of the best scullers in the world, I had to quit tricking myself with excuses.

Much can be said about excuses in sport and in life. In the end — if results are the measure — how little I had trained did not matter. My inkling that Igor disliked me made no difference either. When I did not make the U.S. National Team in 1998, my failure was no one's fault but my own. All my failures have been, at least at the most fundamental level, my own responsibility. In this truth lies an important lesson. Throughout the course of life's various activities, people inevitably encounter adversity that hinders them, delays them and often prevents them from reaching their destination. I should hardly need to give examples of times when setbacks exist in our everyday lives, because they occur so regularly. We catch a red light on the way to work. The pizza deliveryman brings pineapple instead of pepperoni. These are times when we want something one way and the reality turns out another. Certainly we would not consider ourselves failures for missing a green light, or for receiving the wrong pizza. Yet these setbacks occur, all too often. Accordingly, people tend to seek an explanation for their setbacks, and in doing so, frequently attribute blame to someone or something else. It is an absurd game, blaming traffic lights for turning red or for taking too long, but we do it all the time. If it's not the light itself we blame, it's the cautious driver in front of us who doesn't proceed through the yellow light that we also would have passed if she had gone through herself. Even if it isn't a conscious attribution of blame, people can become incensed during frustrating times. We all know frustration arises in the most unexpected moments. It can arise because something turns out contrary to our ambition, because of something beyond our control, because of something within our control or often simply because of life's inauspicious moments. Frustration is only natural, of course, and I am no less guilty of it than anyone else. In the times when I have muffled it and kept my silence or taken a prudent course, I have almost always found that the decision left me far better off than the alternative. What troubles me is when I falsely blame something or someone else for the setbacks that I incur. It would be dishonest with myself to do that with my results in 1998.

When I did not make the U.S. Rowing Team after finishing fifth in the single scull at the Single's Trials, I was frustrated and ready to find some source of blame to account for my loss. People told me that I could blame Igor, who seemed to look for height and strength first in his athletes. Yet, I could no sooner blame Igor than I could blame my oars for being oars or the water for resisting my endurance. There is no place for excuses in athletics or, for that matter, anywhere else. Although I believed I was qualified to participate on the U.S. National Sculling Team, my performance had not been adequate to merit my selection. This did not mean I could not make it in the future. It simply meant that improvement must come from within, and once I began a lifestyle that constantly sought to improve myself, I was certain that success would follow.

When I thought about my options, I realized it was time to make an honest decision. I could either give up my goal of achieving rowing greatness or I could persevere through the obstacles. I had confidence in myself, but without proper action, I was destined to be another mediocre rower who never tapped into his full potential. I had gone and had my fun. Touring with a rock band was the wildest thing I could possibly have done. Now it was time to seek out the best competition; it was time to train with the fastest scullers I could find; and most of all, it was time to step up to the next level. I decided to move to Boston to train with former world champion, Jamie Koven.

       ❖   ❖   ❖   ❖   ❖

Those who row, and those who know the rowing stroke, have a phrase that describes one of the stroke's most important moments. It's called "the catch." The catch is that point when, after sliding forward toward the stern of the boat, with knees bent to the chest and oars feathered toward the bow, the time comes to drop the oars into the water and propel the boat on its way. The moment the oars turn in their oarlocks and the blades face perpendicular to the water, the blades dip beneath the surface of the water, the legs push forward and the oars do their work. It is extremely important at this point of the stroke to have a clean entrance into the water and not disturb the motion of the boat. All of these actions are in an effort to maintain complete efficiency in the transition from recovery to exertion. The moment when the catch takes place can be one of the most unsteady parts of the stroke. Once the oars are in the water, the legs push against the foot stretcher and the boat propels forward as the oarsman suspends his weight on the oars. The catch is a transition point in the stroke and, for good or bad, it can greatly effect the speed of the boat.

I believe there are moments in life similar to the catch of the rowing stroke. These are the times when, after coasting in one direction for some time, we hit a point when it's time to change direction, when it's time to pivot and begin moving our life more firmly on its way. In my life, the catch came in 1998, when I moved to Boston to train with Jamie.

No one needs reminding that we all reach a point when something we do seems as if it might be going the wrong direction. At such crucial moments we are forced to make a number of decisions. Should we continue pursuing the same end? If we do continue, should we do it in a different fashion? Is it time to call it quits? These questions are among life's toughest. There is nothing harder, for instance, than trying to mend a personal relationship that has reached its catch. But at some level, a decision to continue or to turn back must be made. It is in these moments when we ask the most of ourselves as humans. We see what we are all about and answer the most important questions of all: Why do we do what we do, and given our reason for doing what we do, how far are we willing to go to do it? Examining my life made it clear to me that I row because it improves my quality of character and enriches my experience of the world. As regards how far I was willing to go — I was just starting to find that out.

CHAPTER 4

Making My Move

Nelson Mandela once wrote, "There are victories whose glory lies only in the fact that they are known to those who win them." Many of my victories have this private sense of meaning. Some goals in life do not have an outcome that others can observe. While these goals may go unnoticed by all but the person who sets them, they are still important types of goals. Yes, after moving to Boston, I had my aspirations to make the National Team in 1999 and the Olympic Team in 2000, but these were not my only aims. Along the path to reach these more visible and somewhat terminal goals, I had set a number of other objectives for myself. Most immediately, I wanted to become more dependable and more consistent in my life and in my training. Ken Dreyfuss once said to me, "Aquil, you have to be a champion in life before you can be a champion on the water." His words inspired me. I decided to use my intermediary and private objectives as personal tests to ensure that I was on the right course to reach the Olympic games.

It is sometimes useful to remember that each individual is the only one who can monitor his own progress or check his own bearings. Other people can offer their opinions, and many can even be objective in their analysis or coaching, but in the end, each individual must account for his actions by setting high standards based on the goals he wants to achieve. Pretend, for example, that your boss at work wants you to complete a project that will be due in two weeks. Your boss may assign a sequence of deadlines to keep your progress steady and to ensure you complete the final project on time. It is not beyond the

Defeated after the Henley in 1999

"Because this was Aquil's first race at Henley and he may have been
awed by the sense of tradition, he hesitated to ask for enough time to
have his footstretcher properly repaired, which we most certainly
would have given him"
  — Angus Robertson, Henley Race Committee

Photo by Chris Milliman / *The Independent Rowing News*

Me just missing a tackle on a kickoff return at the **1990 DC Championships where Wilson lost to Anacostia.** Representing the Wilson Tigers are #72-John Devall, making the tackle #23-Shon Haigler, on the ground #86 Aquil Abdullah.

John Devlin, my head coach at George Washington University

George Washington Varsity Crew sweeping on the Potomac.

The 1992 GWU Head of the Charles Championship Eight, from bow to stern Eric Monrad, Me, Mike Johnson, Alex Mundt, Tony Spinelli, Prospero (Perky) Gogo, Matt Russell, Tim Downs, (Coach) John Devlin, and (Cox) James Rivera. With a couple of changes and Brian Winke, this boat would go onto become the first Men's Eight at GWU to medal at the Dad Vails.

Coaches Ken Dreyfuss, Dan Lyons, Michael Hughes and the nine Potomac Boat Club Scullers at the **1997 World Championships:** Andy McMarlin, Steve George, Me, Conal Groom, Sean Groom, Kate Ackerman, Olwen Huxley, Kari Hughes, and Megan Taylor.

The 2000 Thames World Sculling Challenge, from right to left Greg Searle, Michael Veberschek, Valcalv Chalupa [?], Itok Cop [?]. Me, and the 2000 winner of the Doggets Coat and Badge. We are just about to draw lanes for the 4.1 mil[e] race that is held the day before the Oxford-Cambridge Boat Race.

Me and Jamie at **The 2000 Power Ten Banquet in New York City,** where Stephen Redgrave was the guest speaker.

At Henley with **Don Spero, former world sculling champion.**
Photo by: Nancy Chasen

With **Canadian great Derik Porter** after the Pan American Games

The race against Don Smith at the **2000 Olympic Trials.**

Photos by: Vicki Valerio / *U.S. Rowing* / *Philadelphia Inquirer*

After the 2000 Olympic Trials Final, Don and I embrace. Mike Teti, Jamie Koven, and my mother look on.

Photo by: Vicki Valerio / *U.S. Rowing* / *Philadelphia Inquirer*

My wonderful mother shows where I got my smile.
Photo by: Merrill McKenzie

Receiving The Pineapple Cup at the 2000 Henley.

"You mean I get to keep this?, said Aquil"
— Angus Robertson, Henley Race Committee

Photo by: Jet Photo

question, if your boss is diligent, for her even to provide clearly delin-
eated smaller objectives within the intermediary goals she already
assigned. Yet, no matter how many attempts your boss makes to keep
you on pace, ultimately, only you can make sure that the work is done,
that it's done right and that it's done on time.

Because each person is the only one accountable for his actions,
each person is also the only one responsible for his success or failure.
If we set a clearly structured system of priorities, we can nourish these
priorities by successfully accomplishing goals along the way. We do so
many things expecting to be compensated in a certain fashion. Having
expectations of reward can be a great motivational force, but in looking too far ahead one can easily forget all that is gained simply in the
process of trying. Rowing is for me a vehicle toward self-improvement.
The sport is the best way I have found to improve and challenge
myself. It would therefore be inappropriate for me to gear my goals
exclusively toward success in rowing when rowing is merely the means
to achieve a greater goal — improving who I am. As I see it, success in
rowing naturally denotes success in life, because the qualities necessary to excel in the sport are the same qualities that make excellent
people: determination, hard work, honesty, dedication, perspective. If
our priorities don't match our goals then we should not be disappointed if we don't reach our goals. For example, when I set my goal as
making the National Team in 1998, but I decided to go on tour with
my band, I should not have been disappointed when I did not race the
speed required to make the team. Nothing speaks of our priorities so
clearly as our actions.

When someone spends an exorbitant amount of time on a particular task, how can one gauge whether that effort is worthwhile? In
particular, if the visible result of such commitment appears to be shy of
the goal, what validation can one find for the effort he or she made?
The straight answer calls upon a cliché we have all heard before: the
journey matters more than the destination. At the most fundamental
level I can furnish no truism as wise as this. And yet, there is something to be said for reaching that final destination and for obtaining
that ultimate prize. All my training may be valuable insofar as it has
brought my persistence, commitment and hard work in athletics to
other aspects of my life, but is it necessarily sweet or even the right
decision? I do not doubt for a moment that our long-fought efforts in
life to reach a certain end are worthwhile, even if we fail to reach our
intermediary goals. But we must examine exactly what our goals

mean, and why we strive to reach them in the first place.

For me, goals are a tangible way to measure myself as a human being. Making the U.S. National Sculling Team is a goal that requires a great deal of hard work and dedication. Rowing is a sport that weeds out those who lack dedication and deliberate effort. Most practices are in the morning before sunrise, and the most serious among us practice again in the afternoons. We adjust our diets to accommodate our rowing fitness, and we lift weights to build bodies sculpted specifically for excellence in our sport. Being an elite rower is a full time occupation that demands a strong quality of human being. Making the men's U.S. National Sculling Team is an accomplishment awarded to only the seven men who best exemplify that special, strong hearted, elite rowing athlete. To make the team would be to prove to myself that I belong among that upper echelon of high-quality people.

Let my message be clear. Not everyone who reaches a high level of success in sports is a high-quality character. I need not mention the swarm of all-star athletes who stand out as bad influences. Rowing does not imply that someone is a "good person," but unlike some professional sports with more national publicity — sports whose athletes fall under media scrutiny for getting into trouble or creating negative attention — crew has generally never been a recreation that breeds people with character foibles and controversial misdeeds. For one, there is no money involved in rowing. Rowers today compete for the love of competition and the joy in moving a boat over water. Second, the lack of publicity given to rowers leaves their personal lives largely unknown to the public. A rower could be a good or a bad person, but that rower at least has a genuine passion and respect for what he does because it comes without riches or fame. The rowing world is often enormous for those who know it and nonexistent for everyone else. Many outstanding people have no inkling what sculling is or whether you use an oar, knife, pen or helmet to do it. Despite the anonymity (or perhaps because of it) dedicated rowers have their own personal and meaningful motives to work hard. My motive in rowing has been to prove to myself that I can stand up to the challenge of being "great." It would take a lot to make America's Sculling Team, but the process would show me how adept I am at honoring the overall priorities in my life.

Moving to Boston was a big step, and different from any decisions in my past. In Boston there were no known variables. I had no boat and no boathouse. Whereas before I had trained under a specific program with specific practice schedules and plans, in Boston I had no coach to guide me. All I knew was that Jamie was one of the best single scullers in the world, and since he was training in Boston, then I should be training in Boston with him. Luckily, I managed to meet some people who helped me find a boat and a boathouse. Buzz Congrum and Carrie Graves, the men's and women's crew coaches at Northeastern University, allowed me to row from their boathouse. Sarah Hall from Resolute Racing Shells arranged for me to row in a Resolute boat. Everything fit together better than I could have hoped.

After Double's Trials, when I returned to Boston, I was the only rower around. Jamie was away at the 1998 World Championships with the National Team, and Cyrus had the opportunity to make the National Team in the pair, when Ted Murphy got injured and Adam Holland needed a partner. I was left to train alone. For the first time it was up to me to get up in the morning and trudge out to the water. There were no groups of rowers to feed my motivation. It all had to come from within. Had I not trained, there would have been no one to tell me to quit slacking. The only one I would have hurt would have been myself. In the past I may have lapsed when faced with this situation, but my attitude had changed.

When I first arrived in Boston I stayed with Alex Selvig, and his house was four or five miles from the Northeastern boathouse. Every morning I rode my bike to Northeastern, unloaded my boat and plopped it down on the water. I then rowed a vast portion of the Charles River, covering around eighteen miles a day from the boathouse to the basin, down to Watertown at the end of the river, then back to Northeastern. In the afternoon I came back on my bike and rowed some more, often until dark. My workouts were strong and challenging. I was excited for Jamie to return and push me even harder. In the fall when Cyrus returned, I moved into an apartment with him and Katie Scanlon. Katie Scanlon rowed in the women's quad in 1998 with Julia Chilicki, Kelly Sahcow and Sarah Field. Katie and Julia had planned to row in the double at the 1998 World Championships, but when they did not win the Trials they jumped into a quad with Kelly and Sarah instead. Both Katie and Julie had been on the National Team in previous years and Julie was one of the fastest single scullers in the country. Along with Cyrus, Julia and Katie would become my family in Cambridge.

When Jamie returned from the World Championships he rowed through the fall season and then told me that he might be taking some time off. *Taking time off*, I thought, *but you're the reason I'm up here!* Jamie did not clarify his reasons. I sensed that a personal problem kept him from the water, but I didn't know him well enough then to discuss it. The first time I met Jamie was in 1995, at the U.S. Nationals held in Gainsville, Georgia. Steve George and Jamie were driving back to Washington together, and I hitched a ride. Jamie and Steve had rowed at Brown University, a school known for producing some of the country's top crews in previous years. Back then I didn't know too much more about Jamie than his reputation on the water. I knew he'd done well at Brown, that he had been on the National Team, and that he pulled a good erg score. The drive to Washington gave us time to get acquainted. By the time I moved to Boston to train with him in 1998, we'd encountered one another on the rowing circuit many times. Still we weren't that close. When he told me he was taking time off, I didn't understand his reason.

Jamie had not done as well as expected at the 1998 World Championships, and there was a lot of speculation as to why. I suspected the explanation had something to do with why he was taking time off. Sure enough, after the fall Head races Jamie told me his back had been bothering him. He would have to take some time to let it heal. Jamie said he was not even certain he would continue his rowing career. Hearing this news left me with mixed emotions. The person I had followed north to train with was telling me he might never row again. *That stinks*, I thought. At the same time, though, Jamie was a friend; I wanted whatever was best for him. Although he didn't broadcast it then, Jamie had a degenerative bone disease that damaged his back severely. For a while I would have to continue training alone. So, with my routine already established, I continued my eighteen mile mornings and twilight sprints every day for at least a month.

Fortunately, I found a job at Moldyn, Inc., located in Cambridge. My previous work for Photon Research Associates positioned me for the job with Moldyn, where I stepped in and immediately participated in some exciting projects. With Moldyn I worked on a project studying multi-body dynamics. They gave me challenging tasks like programming computers and working on algorithms. Between work and training I managed to keep busy, but what I really wanted was Jamie's healthy return so we could start training together.

Rowing alone for a long time was a nice change for me. It helped prove to myself how committed I had become. Nevertheless, I needed different ways to keep interested and challenged other than rowing with no training partner. I joined Mike's Original Gym near my apartment in Cambridge, and tried to think of creative ways to stay in shape. First I started plyometrics, then I began jumping rope, and eventually I began taking ballet and yoga. Yoga was something that Jamie and I could do together since it helped stretch his back. On the mornings when it was too cold to row on the Charles, I rode my bike through three feet of snow to the gym, where I could train on the ergometer. People in the gym would sit next to me rowing on another erg and they would look at me and try to correct my form. "You're doing that wrong," they would say, trying to help. Whether or not my skin color made people think I didn't know the proper rowing form, I cannot say. Certainly my form is far from perfect. It always struck me as funny though, that people who didn't know the first thing about the rowing stroke would try to help me improve mine. Between using the gym for weights, taking the ballet classes to improve my agility and doing yoga with Jamie, I found plenty of non-rowing activities to keep my interest and fitness where they needed to be.

When Jamie came back to the water in late January of 1999, I was ready for his return. In addition to his back ailment, Jamie had other important events going on in his life. He was getting married, and with his approaching wedding came a slew of practical concerns that kept him from the water. Once we started training together, he must have felt a great relief at the release rowing can provide for the stress and pressure that accumulate in other areas of life. I was relieved that my primary reason for coming to Boston was finally able to join me.

Jamie and I had no one to guide us. We had each been coached before, so we knew how to execute the rowing stroke. But with no one to correct our technical deficiencies on a day-to-day basis, it was up to us to design and adhere to a training regimen that would make us as fit as possible. Jamie and I would have to take the foundations we'd acquired through our past coaches and build from them on our own. Jamie was the perfect partner with whom to do so. I had wanted to seek out the best sculler I could find, and Jamie, who had been the world champion in 1997, was the best around. Great instructors Steve Gladstone, Mike Spraklin and Scott Roop had coached him, and he had also successfully trained on his own. Jamie was a constant challenge for me to improve.

Training in Boston reminded me of Sylvester Stallone in *Rocky IV*, sweating through a montage of intense exertion. I'd thought that DC could get cold in the winter, but compared to Boston, winter in DC was like being on a tropical island. My life in Boston moved at much the same pace as in all the places I had trained: I rowed, I worked, I rowed. The only difference was that this time there was no one to catch me if I fell. If I failed to improve no one would have asked what happened to Aquil. I would have just disappeared from the radar screen into the deep abyss of "rowers that never were."

The people at Moldyn, Inc. allowed me to train as much as I wanted provided I got my work done. When I couldn't make enough money to make ends meet, I worked weekend shifts at Olympic Moving and Storage. Life was tough, but I didn't have anything else to do, so I figured there was no need to complain.

On a day-to-day level, Jamie and I chose workouts that we thought would challenge us. There was no special formula to our plan. We would do 3x10 minutes and 1x7 minutes on Monday, steady state rowing on Tuesday, 3x20 minutes on Wednesday, steady, long rows on Thursday, and 600 hard strokes on Friday. On Saturday we would go into the grab bag and do something like 2000 meter pieces or 20 minutes pieces depending on the time of year. Nothing magical characterized our training. I spent more time on the erg than I had since college, and I made a point to lift weights more consistently than before. The general goal of it all was to improve our style, speed, efficiency and endurance. If we met these objectives we would meet our larger goals and in meeting those we would fulfill the greater ones we held as priorities over them all.

There are many advantages of training with someone who has similar objectives as one's own, but most of all, I think, the advantage lies in the opportunity to be pushed by another person in a way that exceeds the level we can ever push ourselves while alone. Competition makes for higher intensity and thus fosters improvement. Jamie and I always tried to compete with one another in a friendly fashion (though I can only remember one practice when we didn't clash oars or yell at each other out of mutual encouragement). Rowing side by side pushed us each that extra bit harder.

When we first began, Jamie's speed over the water was so much greater than my own that I always took a head start when we rowed our pieces together. That way we could each row our hardest and he would catch me at a point in the race when we could challenge one another to finish first. Most of our training proceeded like this, rowing pieces of various lengths and pushing one another as best we could while I took the lead necessary to make it an evenly matched challenge. A few months passed, the season changed over Boston, and the Charles River became familiar to me like the Potomac waters I knew from home. We were working hard: twice a day on the water, in the weight room three days a week and inside on the erg just slightly less.

One day, out on the water, on a clear morning with blue skies and crisp air, Jamie and I took position for one of our 2000 meter pieces. I started rowing up ahead, taking my normal lead so we could begin as usual, when Jamie said: "You don't need to do that anymore." The words surprised me. I stopped rowing and realized he was right. Months of training in a system of constant challenge improved me to a level I had never been before. Jamie still defeated me consistently, but it was no longer a given that he would prevail. In all of the time we had trained, I hadn't noticed that I had been holding him off longer, and that he wasn't allowing me to start as far ahead of him. It wasn't until that day, when I looked over at him and then down the course to check my point, that I realized I was getting faster. Jamie was one of the world's best scullers, and on that day, for the first time, I realized that I could hold my own with him. I'd trained my way to compete evenly among America's best.

One reason for my sudden ability to stay with Jamie was the head start I had while he nursed his injury. Another reason, I think, is the slight difference in our training routine. Since I had no car I had to ride my bike everywhere. Jamie trained from Riverside boathouse, only a few minutes from where he lived. I continued to train from Northeastern boathouse, several miles from my home and at least three miles down the river from Riverside. Every morning we met at the Boston University bridge, which meant that in addition to the longer commute to the boathouse, I also had to row an additional three miles just to meet Jamie at the start of our workout. Usually when we met Jamie wouldn't be warmed up, so while he warmed up I would put in even more extra strokes. Though my longer bike ride and extra strokes may seem like a small deal from a daily perspective, it all amounted to that extra bit of training that helped me reach Jamie's level.

As the winter of 1999 progressed to the spring, a new season of rowing began. This would be my showcase year. I hoped for a chance to prove that my work had been worthwhile. The 1999 National Team Trials in Augusta were coming up that summer, but before the Trials I would have yet another chance to see where I stood among some of the best scullers in the country. The Speed Order race would be just the test.

That spring, Don Smith went out on the water with us a few times, but other than that, I had no idea how I compared with outside competition. Don was in school at Wharton, so his time training on the water with me and Jamie was somewhat sporadic. Usually Jamie won the pieces when the three of us competed. Don won a few, and on occasion I would win. Beyond those races though, I was blind to where I stood. The spring Speed Order race in Aiken, South Carolina was where all of the top scullers in the country gathered together to race in a scrimmage. It was there that I would have the chance to see what my hard work had wrought.

The first part of the spring Speed Order usually consists of a 2000 meter ergometer test. I had never been very good on the ergometer. Most elite heavyweight rowers could break six minutes, and I had never broken 6:10. I knew that I was mentally ready and physically prepared to do better than I had ever done. Sure enough, when we made it down to Aiken and the time came to test, I rowed a 6:06. The time was my personal best, but still much slower than the top score of 5:52. Unfortunately, the erg scores determined the heats for the races on the water, and I was in the third tier of erg scores.

On race day, I found myself anxious to compete against someone other than Jamie or Don for the first time in almost five months. I knew that none of the people I would race would be as fast as them, but I didn't know if anyone else would be as fast as me. The starter's flag dropped and I went out with my normal start, twenty strokes at a high rating. When I settled into my race rhythm I stayed focused on what was going on in my boat. Head up, shoulders relaxed, legs down. *Keep it simple.* When I looked to my side at the 1500 meter mark there was no one close to me. Of all the heats, I had the fastest time. By the end of the Speed Order I had beaten everyone at the race, including Don. So it remained that I had only Jamie to beat, and I had one month to catch him before the Trials.

My training in Boston made the 1999 Trials an entirely different affair from the years before. Not only would my level of success be better, but the perception other people in the rowing community had of me would change as well. By moving to Boston, I showed everyone that I was serious about becoming America's top single sculler. There remained some skepticism about my ability to compete at that upper tier, and now that everyone knew I had made the commitment to try, my talent would be put to the test. No one — myself included — could any longer say that I might have a chance at greatness if only I would train harder. This was one of those unknown victories Nelson Mandela wrote of so wisely.

In athletics, as in other parts of life, I believe I owe it to myself to seek whatever situations and circumstances I can to make the most out of my endeavors. How else does one maximize potential? During some of my time with Potomac Boat Club, my dedication was unsteady. Since then I've improved it. After training with Jamie in 1998 and the start of 1999, it was crucial for me, privately, to make a visible improvement in my racing performance over the previous years. I had reached the point where I could no longer tolerate my failures. As a response, I worked hard to maximize that potential. After training with Jamie, I had not one doubt about how hard or how persistently I had trained. It would come down to talent and timing, because I had done all I could have done to make myself the best I could be.

The month leading up to the Trials placed some strain on the friendly relationship that Jamie and I had on the water. Both of us were gearing up for the same race with the same goal. There was a little more tension in our practices, neither of us wanting to yield to the other. I started to get annoyed at Jamie when he beat me; soon the accusations of who was cheating on the last piece began to fly with fury.

I decided to head south a little early and go for a tune-up session on the Potomac with Ken Dreyfuss. While Charlie Butt Jr. and John Riley had kindly provided some technical advice in Boston, coaching of that sort was the exception more than the rule. I was happy to get some direct instruction on the mechanics of my stroke. It was also necessary to get away from the intensity of training with Jamie. Washington was an environment where I could clearly focus on my rowing style. Ken had me slow everything down and then speed it back up, urging me to move the shell faster without rowing harder. We both knew that I was as fit as I had ever been, but what I had to do now was use that fitness as efficiently as possible.

I arrived in Augusta with the usual fanfare. I made a stop at The Dock, a store owned by Kathy Stitt, the local den mother in Augusta. She gave me a hug, asked me how I had been and made small talk. Strangely, my focus then surpassed my focus at any other regatta I had participated in, and I didn't hang out like usual. After my visit with Kathy, I went back to Chris Duffy's apartment, where I was staying, and started to prepare myself for the week ahead.

For the 1998 Trials, I had shared a hotel room with Jamie, and I learned a lot. Jamie would wake up about three to four hours before the race and then go for a run, come back to the hotel and stretch out. We would then get a small bite to eat and hang out in the hotel until we were ready to leave for the course. In 1999 I would follow the same routine, only this time I would do it alone.

Jamie was the top seed at the regatta, and perennial favorites such as Cyrus Beasley and Don Smith were not rowing in the single. I was seeded second. It was no secret that there was only one person at the regatta who was likely to be faster than I was, and I knew him all too well. Other oarsmen present had earned my respect — guys like Ian McGowan, Nick Peterson, Mike Ferry, Will Fisher and Chris Duffy — but of all the people on the water, only Jamie had a real chance of beating me. The races were drawn with both of us on opposite sides of the bracket. We each progressed as planned through our heats and semi-finals. It was not until the first final that we met.

The first final unfolded in an unexpected manner. Mike Ferry pushed out to a strong start. *How long could he keep that up?* I wondered. I stuck to my plan. *Steady drive. Wait for the surge.* Jamie was right there with me. *Steady.* Mike started losing steam. Jamie and I passed him. We were bow-to-bow. With 600 meters left in the race, Jamie began to pull ahead. I tried to go with him but my legs stalled; they just wouldn't go down fast enough. *Push!* I told myself. *Push and swing!* But my legs wouldn't do the job. I managed to hold on and finish a little under 3 seconds behind him. How close I came in second place didn't matter. In a best of three final series, Jamie had a distinct advantage by winning on the first day. After that, if I didn't come to race on Sunday, all would be lost. When we left the water, I cooled down, put my boat away and left the racecourse thinking about what I needed to do to win.

Psychologically, there is a lot at stake in athletics, and particularly so when slated against a competitor who one knows well. It is natural to view our competitors as adversaries, but in this case, Jamie had become my close buddy. I could hardly view him as an enemy. When training with someone, one becomes familiar with the nuances of his partner's personality and work habits. After conditioning in Boston, I knew Jamie both on and off the water. I understood the details of his stroke just as I could name his favorite pancake mix and how he liked his microwave omelet. I knew that he was relentless in his attack; I knew that he was confident in his ability to win; and, I knew that if I were going to win, I really had to believe that I would. As the tunnel of focus narrowed, I tried to put Jamie out of my mind and focus on what *I* was going to do to win the race. Easier said than done. There I was at the 1999 Trials, asked to compete against a close friend, asked to sever all emotional ties and square off in a battle to determine which one of us would reap the rewards of the training we had performed together in equal measure over the majority of the prior year. That's a tough challenge. In an event so individually oriented as single sculling, I had never really taken the time to ponder how we view our competitors. I always felt that my success was up to me, and that my competitors didn't really stand in my way, so much as they jostled by my side, vying for the same goal. Once I was up against a close friend, my perspective changed.

Competing against Jamie was difficult because there was no mysterious element behind his training. Unlike other competitors with whom I did not interact every day, I could not imagine that Jamie had not worked as hard as I, or that he did not have the talent that I possessed. Instead, I knew almost everything that he had done in the previous year to reach the finals, and I had done most of it with him. My mind fought between wanting his success and wanting my own. Naturally the desire for my own victory took precedence. In other sports, perhaps, I would look upon him as more of an opponent who must be obliterated in order to advance myself. If it were football, for example, we would face across the line of scrimmage and battle until one person went down and the other prevailed. That was not the nature of rowing. Crew was far more independent. On the water one could only take care of oneself; there was no way — save through mental intimidation — to affect an opponent's performance. I wanted the distinction of winning the Trials and earning my place on the National Team for the first time, but Jamie did not hinder my attempts. In actuality, he had been the one person who, over several months, most *helped* in my attempt to reach the top. When we sat poised in our boats ready to start the second final, I looked across at Jamie and realized that no matter what happened, we would both be winners.

Langley Pond in Aiken, South Carolina was unusually placid for that second final of the 1999 National Team Trials. In order to win, I would have to get ahead of Jamie early and be in a position to watch his every move and try to respond. Some rowers crack when the race seems hopeless, but I knew that on this day my opponent would not give up. He probably believed himself the better rower, just as I believed the same about myself. Knowing I had to do something drastic to win, when the race began, I jumped out to a nice lead and sustained it through the 1000 meter mark. The strokes came easily. They were hard, strong strokes, but they came with the ease of one who believes he can truly succeed. *Confidence Aquil, confidence.* With every stroke I hoped that Jamie was beginning to doubt himself. Then at 750 meters remaining he made a move. Out burst the confident Jamie I had tried so hard to thwart. *You can still do this Aquil. Believe it.* Going into the last 500 meters I had a slight lead. We each pulled and grimaced. Then it happened: Jamie moved through me. Although I refused to relent, pushing my hardest to stay even, with 300 meters to go Jamie made a final move that I was unable to counter. He held on to win by 1.5 seconds.

Having the opportunity to race against Jamie in the finals proved to me that hard work has positive results. I didn't win as I'd wanted, but something good had still occurred. I had come a long way to reach a time when I was on equal footing with a sculler like Jamie. While the final race of the National Trials was my chance to take a step up, it was also a race we had both already won by improving ourselves enough to make it there. My disappointment weighed me down, but it came with no resentment or hard feelings. At least I had the pleasure of knowing that I had demanded the most of myself and that I had performed at a level I had never performed at before. It can be difficult to take comfort in such intangible consolations. The bottom line was, another year had passed, another National Team Trial was over and I still had yet to make the National Team in the single. Where could I go from there? What more could I do? I received an invitation from Igor to train in Augusta where I could try to earn a spot on the National Team in the quad. Thinking that — more than in any other year — I was in a position to make the team, I accepted Igor's offer.

Then on the first day of quad camp, Igor announced that he had devised a new formula to select team boats. The first part of the formula was ergometer performance record; the second was performance at Trials; and the third component was prior experience in team boats. I will be the first person to admit that the losers in team boat selection usually complain about the fairness of selection procedure. I don't want to complain, but there I was, having just finished my best U.S. National Single's Trials to date, also having won in the double with

Nick Peterson at the Speed Order race, and Igor changed the system. Rowing the erg is important; I cannot deny that. But after the Trials where I proved myself to be several lengths better than the next fastest single sculler, I thought my performance on the water would be given more weight. How wrong I was. Igor put me in the third quad with Garret Klugh, Sean Hall and Nick McQuaid. Garret and Sean had done well in the double, and Nick McQuaid was rowing well then, too. Each of us was trying to figure out how Igor's magical formula made sense if the guys who appeared to have done the best were placed in the worst boat at the camp.

When we went out to row some pieces, sure enough, our boat won. We could not possibly have lost. Then Igor started to change the boats around, mixing the seats to try different combinations. No matter what quad configuration he tried, I was not switched from the third boat. Whether my erg scores hurt me in Igor's new formula or if he just didn't want me in his quad, I have no idea. But after a week of rowing in the third quad, and following many long conversations with other coaches and friends, I decided that it was time to leave Augusta. I knew I was one of the best single scullers in America. Whether or not Igor believed I could move a team boat made no difference to me. It was time to test myself against the best from outside the United States. If I couldn't do that at the World Championships, I would try elsewhere. I decided to row in Europe and at the Pan American Games Trials in Indianapolis.

After winning the U.S. National Team Single's Trials Jamie decided to forego the opportunity to row at the Pan American Games. He said that he didn't want to disrupt his training for the World Championships by participating in the closely scheduled Pan American Games. Since I would not be going to the World Championships with the U.S. National Team, I had no reason *not* to try to participate in the Pan American Games. After I left Augusta I went to train in Boston for the Pan American Trials.

Once the Pan Am Trials arrived I was still rowing well. The races were not very exciting, though they turned out much more difficult than I intended. Will Fisher and Nick McQuaid put up tough efforts in the finals, but I emerged the winner. The victory was good for me. Since I had performed as expected there was not much celebration surrounding the accomplishment. The win gave me a berth in the upcoming Pan American Games, but before they arrived I was off for Europe — to race in the 1999 Henley Royal Regatta, and the World

Cup Regatta at Lucerne.

The days between regattas are preserved in my memory as extra folds in time, as small bubbles enabling me to catch up with friends, take a deep breath and prepare to keep moving forward. When the Pan Am Trials ended, I spent a day with a close friend of mine from college named Emily Wilis. She had tickets to see Dave Matthews, and we were just able to see the show before I had to catch a plane to New York. In New York I had another day of down time before I left for Europe. Since I would need a blue blazer for the Henley, I called another college friend named Mercedes McAndrews, and together we went shopping. In a quick whirl, the next day I met fellow oarsmen Dan Debonis and Will Fisher at JFK airport, and we boarded a plane for London.

I was excited for the upcoming European regattas. Each would offer the chance to test myself against international competition that I had never had the opportunity to face. The decision to row in Europe did not come easily, for it represented another signal that I was putting my skills on the line by exposing myself to the greater rowing world. Unfortunately, my performances did not turn out as I had hoped. After breaking my foot-stretchers at Henley, I wanted to redeem myself at the final leg of the Rowing World Cup in Lucerne.

The World Cup Regatta in Lucerne was usually the last race before the World Championships, and as such it served as a good indicator of where people were in their training. I had thought Henley was a nice place to row, but Lucerne was better still. Lake Lucerne sat nestled between mountain peaks and surrounded by green pastures where cows grazed with bells around their necks. The city had an enchanting charm about it and the people were friendly. At one end of the course was an area designated for gambling. Millions of dollars weren't at stake, but the wagers were enough to add some excitement. Across from the gambling area was a spectator's seating section that looked out over the course and had in full view an enormous screen that televised the action on the water.

Originally, after the Royal Henley Regatta, I planned to stay at Henley-on-Thames for a couple of days then travel to Lucerne rather than go all the way back to the United States for the brief week between regattas. Then I learned that the U.S. Team had room for me to stay with them in their hotel, and I left with them ahead of plan. Although I hadn't finished first in the U.S. National Team Trials that year, I represented the United States at the World Cup in the sense that each country was allowed to enter two boats per event, and the United States only had Jamie as the single sculler competing. Because I had won the Pan American Trials and would represent the United States Rowing Team in the Pan American Games, I was technically a part of the U.S. Team. But at the World Cup Regatta in Lucerne, U.S. Rowing did not fund my trip. I had to raise the money through other means. Fortunately, I have always had generous benefactors to help me. My European trip was funded with the help of Team Potomac 2000, Knickerbocker Management and the National Rowing Foundation. Several people were behind the scenes making my trip happen. Finn Casperson, Don Spero, Paul Knight, Eric Meyers, Hart Perry and Mike Teti helped immeasurably. Then once I was abroad, U.S. Rowing was generous enough to take me into their fold even though I was not officially a member of the National Team. I had no idea where I would be staying in Lucerne, but thanks to Willie Black and Mark Sniderman, I was able to stay in the hotel with the rest of the U.S. contingent.

Boyd Lytle from Resolute Racing Shells arranged for me to row in a Resolute boat at both the Henley and Lucerne regattas, but I did not communicate with him before I left Henley, so in the days prior to the Lucerne Regatta, I trained in a Stampfli shell. Ken Dreyfuss from Potomac Boat Club had arranged for me to row the Stampfli. Without his help I would have been swimming instead of rowing, because I didn't have the money to pay for a boat. Team Potomac 2000 reimbursed Ken, but the generosity saved me because the Resolute boat did not arrive until the day before my race. Even though I was accustomed to the Resolute shell, I did not want to switch from a boat that I had been racing in all week prior to the race.

On the day of my first race, everything was settled. I had a boat and rowed in a heat to determine the best boats that would advance. Never before had I been pushed by such great competition. Although the Henley was the first real big international race that I had competed in, not every good sculler participated at Henley. On the other hand, the World Cup Regatta at Lucerne had some of the world's best oarsmen. In my heat were several accomplished scullers, including the eventual winner of the regatta and an Egyptian rower who had consistently made the finals in previous years. It did not really occur to me when I faced Ali Ibriham, the Egyptian, that I was racing against another person of dark skin, although we must have stood out among the others. In my first race of the regatta I was pushed from the start.

I did not qualify, but I did beat Ali. After that I was placed in the repecharge.

In the repecharge race later that day the course moved quickly. The best oarsmen had already advanced, but the oarsmen remaining weren't exactly chumps. *No sense leaving anything behind,* I thought. *Might as well give it all I can.* But even with that attitude I was challenged to win. The challenge was good for me, and win I did, advancing to the semi-final on the following day.

For the semi-final I wanted to get out to a strong start and make my move early. If I advanced I would race against Jamie Koven in the finals. After training with Jamie and facing him in the U.S. National Team Trials, we shared plenty of competitive experience. But another match was not meant to be. I lost the semi-final race and ended my first international efforts on a low note. Failing to meet my expectations not only let me down, it also made me feel as though others had lost some confidence in my ability. The experience in Europe showed me that I had a long way to go until I would be on the starting line racing for the gold. As much as I had trained, there was still more to be done. Without even a pause to ponder my performance, I returned to Princeton and trained for one last competition — the Pan American Games.

In Princeton, nothing much changed. I trained against a lightweight women's double and got some coaching from many time U.S. single sculling champion, Jim Dietz. The summer of racing had taken its toll on my body and spirits. My weight was down under 180 pounds and the hot and humid summer days of Princeton sometimes made training a chore instead of a pleasure. I found solace in reminding myself that I had just one more race before the summer was over. Everyone remembers the last race.

Finally, the day to leave Princeton arrived. All the rowers going to Canada for the Games loaded into a mini-van headed to Newark Airport. The Pan American Games are a lot like the Olympics for countries in the Americas. Small countries that don't have the money to race all over the world will often compete in the Pan American Games that occur every four years on the year prior to the Olympics. Although there would be some very good single scullers at the Pan Am Games, the competition would not be as fierce as it had been at the World Cup Final in Lucerne. We were ready for gold. Mike Teti, the U.S. men's sweep coach, came over to the mini-van and rested his hands on the window. He looked at all of the guys in the back seat who were sweep rowers, and said, "If you lose, don't bother coming back."

"What about me, Mike?" I asked.

He looked at me through the window and said, "Aquil, just don't under perform."

As we pulled out of the Princeton parking lot and I thought about Mike's departing words, I tried to figure out what he was saying. I came to the conclusion that his message to me was the same as his message to the sweep guys: we were all prepared to race and race well. If we all performed as we were capable — not just how we were expected to perform — then the eight would win and I would finish no lower than second.

Nothing compares to participating in an athletic endeavor as a representative of one's country. The colors on one's racing jersey symbolize the dream of every American oarsman. Rowing on the United States National Team, I competed against oarsmen from other countries who each wanted to bring success and fame back to their homeland. During the opening ceremonies the different nations attended in wondrous uniforms, bearing flags held proudly and high. The U.S. Rowing Team had nominated me as the U.S. flag bearer. The captains from each team in all the different sports elect a person to carry the flag at the opening ceremonies. The intent is to select the athlete who best represents the character of American Sport. Although the members of the rowing contingent nominated me as the U.S. Rowing flag bearer candidate, I soon found that other athletes from different sports had far more incredible stories in their rise to athletic glory. My troubles were few compared to some others who had undergone far more difficult experiences than the dismissal of a coach, or being one of the first men in U.S. rowing with black skin. Every person there was special for what he or she had accomplished. My battle was no more remarkable than that of anyone else. My own hang-ups and failures had been the only obstacle that ever really stopped me from being all that I wanted. Nothing and no one else could be blamed.

I felt like I had worked hard to place myself in a situation where I could reap the rewards of my hard work. Being among other athletes who felt the same way was reward enough in itself. Everyone there seemed proud to represent something bigger than his or her individual goals. Although the games were competitive, the participants seemed to find camaraderie among their differences. Someone once mentioned to me that it must be a strange change, at events like the Pan American games, to compete against other people of black skin. To be honest, it never occurred to me.

My nomination as flag bearer ended with other nominees who were far more qualified. My skin color had not been a big barrier for me, though many suppose it has. Truth told, I have not spent much time pondering the issue of race in the rowing community. The only race I was ever concerned with was the one I was in: the race on the water. People in America perceive the sport of rowing as an elite, white, upper class sport when the reality is more diverse than people suppose. Undeniably, the sport is still inaccessible to a lot of people. To row, one needs some water to row on and some exposure to those who are among the sport's most successful. Many people do not have these opportunities. The sport's financial requirements make rowing even more inaccessible. Equipment is expensive, and traveling to all the regattas empties the wallet quickly. The truth is that I am not poor, but I am not rich either. In all my time rowing I have never missed a race because I couldn't find the money or resources. Supporters of rowing make it possible for those willing to work hard. Wherever there is an earnest desire to row, rowing is possible.

For me, the obstacles came from within. I underwent a long struggle to become comfortable with myself and who I am as a black man. A lot of this struggle I engaged at George Washington University. After I came to terms with myself, being a rower atypical for my skin color no longer bothered me. When I'm out there on the water sitting across from someone who is going to work just as hard as me — someone who will exert the same amount of energy and effort, who will stop at nothing to be the best he can be — then that's all that matters. When I'm training and things are going poorly and my training partner pushes me to not cave in, that's when I know what's most important. People who say, "I'm not prejudiced, I have black friends" are the ones I worry about. The friends closest to me are just good people. The rowers I compete with are just good rowers. They aren't white friends, or black friends, or good white rowers or good black rowers; they're just people like me.

In the Pan American Games I advanced to the finals. There I rowed against the Canadian single sculler, Derik Porter. Derik Porter is a rowing great. He was a member of the Canadian eight that won the gold medal in the Barcelona Olympics, and in 1993 Derik won the gold medal at the World Championships in the single scull. Reaching the finals and facing Derik allowed me to judge myself against an elite rower from outside the United States. Derik had finished third in Lucerne, so I knew what kind of talent I was up against. All boats came out strong at the start. The single sculler from Cuba had more speed than I think anyone expected. He set the pace for the entire first half of the race. At the 1000 meter mark, Derik made his move. As if he had just been waiting to press the button that would send him to victory, Derik surged ahead to a commanding lead. I stayed close, closer than the others, but could not catch him. Derik could probably have finished with a greater lead, but he beat me by a margin of only a few seconds. Finishing second convinced me that I still had what it takes to fulfill my larger goal. I didn't under perform, and my larger goal was just around the bend.

❖   ❖   ❖   ❖   ❖

As may be apparent, particularly in 1998 and 1999, my career in rowing has followed on a wave-like course, riding high through victory and sinking low through defeat. I suppose this is the norm for most athletes. I would even suppose it to be the norm for most people as they go through life doing the things that they do. Certainly some people will tend to ride the crest of the wave more consistently than others do. Likewise some will spend a long time stuck in the trough. Although up to that point in my life I had been a successful oarsman, and undoubtedly I had improved my skills along the way, there was still a long way for me to go.

Now my focus would be the Olympics, that ever-looming goal that stands in the back of every rower's mind. I'd missed my chance in 1996, and I'd been on the brink of the World Championships since then, but making the 2000 Olympic Team was the real goal I'd been aiming for all along. It was the final leg in a marathon journey, and despite the smaller objectives spotted sporadically throughout the course, the big one waited just up ahead.

CHAPTER 5

Six Minutes, Fifty-One Seconds

The 2000 Olympic games were the twenty-third Olympics to include rowing. In Sydney, rowers represented the third largest athlete contingent in the games, behind only track and field and swimming. Despite this size, earning a place on the U.S. Olympic Rowing Team was a challenging task. It meant a lot to a lot of people. In an amateur sport like rowing, when there is little glory and fame on a daily level, there is probably no accomplishment that holds as much value as winning an Olympic medal. Just making the Olympic Team is amazing in itself. While I certainly aspired to win the gold, I first had to accomplish a task I had been unable to do before. I had to earn a place on the National Team.

My 1999 rowing season ended with a second place finish behind Derik Porter at the Pan American Games. After the Pan American Games, I returned to Princeton to get myself ready for the upcoming year. I trained with Jamie as he prepared for the World Championships, and after the team left to compete, I remained in Princeton, where I trained just enough to stay in shape. With nothing else to do, I decided to drive up to Canada to watch the team compete in the World Championships in St. Catherines. The 1999 World Championships were somewhat of a disappointment in that the U.S. Team failed to qualify four boats for the Olympics, which meant that those boats would have to qualify in Lucerne at another Olympic qualifying regatta. When the World Championships ended, I took a vacation in Canada with Laryssa Biesenthal of the Canadian women's eight. The vacation was restful, and it gave me time to get away from rowing — something I had not done in a while.

Rested after a good break, I had to decide what to do next. Each year, Mike Teti, the U.S men's sweep coach, receives hundreds of calls from people who want to come and train in Princeton. I figured that since Mike hadn't asked me to leave, and since I was already living in Princeton, I might as well stay. Early in the 1999 rowing season Mike and I had discussed the possibility that I might train there. During an Olympic year, he wanted to explore and maximize the potential of all possible team candidates. Mike's only request was that I continue to improve. The Princeton Training Center was the best place to prepare for the Olympic Trials that would arrive late in the summer of 2000. Coach Teti's unbending policy of demanding hard work would be just the structure I needed to make sure I never lapsed in my quest to make the National Team. Even though I was a long shot to make the Olympics, I was nevertheless offered the opportunity to train in Princeton among athletes who, in my view, were more qualified than I was.

A number of opportunities made my transition into life in Princeton easier. I was offered a place to stay where I would not have to spend a fortune for rent. Father Tom Mullelly, a local Catholic priest, housed several of the rowers who trained in Princeton. The Catholic diocese in that area owns an eight-bedroom mansion where German author Thomas Mann once lived and physicist Albert Einstein often visited. As a physics major at George Washington, I rather fancied the idea of living in a building once frequented by one of science's greatest geniuses. Anything would have done, of course, and Father Tom, or "FT" as we call him, made me and the other rowers who lived there feel welcome and comfortable. Many of the rowers who lodged in various places throughout the house were not religious at all, and FT did not press Catholicism on any of those who were not interested. He did, however, provide an atmosphere of love and a strong tone of morality that served to enrich the time when we were not training or working. He tried tirelessly to make us feel as though we were members of the Princeton community.

I don't know what I expected to find at the Princeton Training Center (PTC). I think I expected to find the Holy Grail of rowing. The PTC had been so successful in turning out medals that I thought that once I got there I would instantly be good. I thought that there was some secret that Mike Teti had to turn mortal men into rowing gods. The rowing world is full of legends about Mike Teti, some accurate, some taken out of context. The truth is that Mike is a good coach who will yell at his athletes, but only if they make mistakes. If you give him a reason, he will give you a legitimate opportunity, and then he will make you work harder than you've ever worked before. It would take me more than a year to realize that the secret to the PTC was not just the act of a single man, but the act of a group of people united in the pursuit of a single goal: excellence in the sport of rowing. The bottom line about training in Princeton is that you show up for practice, you row, you go to work, and then you train again in the afternoon. In the Olympic year we sometimes trained three times a day. Ultimately, though, I found there was no secret to the success of the PTC — maybe that was the secret.

My life in Princeton was different from most of the guys training at the Center. Most athletes there were in consideration for a team boat, and they knew it. On the other hand, I knew where I stood, and I never fell under the illusion that Mike considered me for a team boat. As a result of this attitude, there was no special attention paid to me. I did not have a specific coach; I did not have a tailor-made training schedule; I didn't even have to show up for practice. No one would mention my absence, except my friend and mentor Mike Porterfield. This lack of attention bothered me at first. I thought that I had come to Princeton to train under the expert eye of Coach Teti, and then I looked around at all the world champions who I trained with, and I realized that they weren't complaining. They were just working hard. Once I stopped thinking about what I *didn't* have at the PTC, and started thinking about what I *did* have instead, immediately I began to improve.

There are many different philosophies to training elite athletes. Some coaches load their athletes' training programs with tons of practice, which is fine when you have athletes who can do nothing but row all day. But when you have athletes who must get home to their wife and kids, or who must be at the office by 9 a.m., then coaches must take another approach to training. As a coach, one must devise a training program that gets the most out of the athletes for the time that the athletes are able to devote. This is the training philosophy implemented at the Princeton Training Center. At the PTC, we trained hard, but we did not train for eight hours a day.

The greatest benefit of training in Princeton was that so many rowers who had already reached the top surrounded me. There is a great comfort in knowing that one has the ability to train alone and succeed, but there is no substitute for competition when trying to push oneself to the next level. Someone once told me of an old experiment conducted by social psychologists in which a man was timed riding his bicycle alone at full speed around a track. He was then timed again, with another cyclist racing by his side. In the second race he performed significantly better, even though he was asked to exert the same energy in both races. In Boston I had Jamie to help increase my intensity, but in Princeton I had dozens of people to match up against, so I worked even harder. Never have I been more fit or more challenged over a long course of time than in preparation for the Olympic Trials.

There were so many people training in Princeton that we had to train in shifts. It is amazing to think that a staff of four coaches trained over sixty athletes. Usually, the larger boats rowed in the early shift and the small boats rowed in the late shift. We moved to this schedule early in the winter, and I rowed with either the women's pair of Missy Ryan and Karen Kraft, or with the men's pairs. With everyone else training for team boats, I had no other single sculler against whom to gauge my speed. I began to gauge my speed by the men's pair — a boat usually faster than the men's single. The tactic worked well for me, because it forced me to compare myself against the best pairs in the country. No matter how hard they were rowing, if I wanted to stay ahead in a workout, I would have to row harder.

As hard as I worked, life at the PTC was not all about training. Proof can be seen in the number of ex-rowers who still live in and around the area, even though their rowing careers are finished. For me, filling my non-training time came easily. Monitor Capital Advisors offered me a job where I could challenge myself intellectually and attempt to advance my career. My employers hired me with the understanding that my real full-time work was training to row. They gave me the freedom to work what hours I could around my rowing schedule, and they offered me the chance to take on only those projects that I felt I could complete. Given the load of my athletic commitment, the freedom to work around rowing was an incredibly propitious blessing. Everything was going just right.

A typical day of training started out in the morning at 6:30 a.m. After waking, I stumbled half asleep to the Princeton University boathouse on Lake Carnegie. One of the coaches would tell us what we were doing and where we were starting. If I were rowing in the single, I would put my boat in the water and warm up by rowing to the meeting place. Sometimes Mike Porterfield would slow his boat down and tell me not to stop at the front end of the stroke, but most of the time he would drive right by me. Occasionally I would be in a team boat, and Coach Teti would holler at me over the water to correct my steering, but most of the time he too would drive right past. By giving these details, I do not mean to say that I received no coaching, just that no one held my hand. Practice started once I reached the meeting point. A few strokes later I would shake off the sleep and start sweating. Once again I would find my routine. Practice ended when one of the coaches called, "Last piece!" The morning workout, in total, lasted about an hour and forty-five minutes, but my day was not over with that.

After rowing, I would usually return to the Aquinas Institute and eat breakfast. In the winter when I was feeling extremely zealous, I would either run or do a small weight session after rowing. These extra workouts were the additional effort that I thought I needed in order to have an edge on everyone else. When lifting weights, I used exercises specifically geared to strengthen those muscles used most in the rowing stroke. My workouts with the weights alternated between shoulders, back, arms and legs. Rather than build a disproportionate physique, I also interspersed some exercises for the remaining muscle groups in my body. Once I was done lifting, running or eating, I would arrive at work around 10:30 a.m. Early in the afternoon, I would cut out of work and return to the boathouse for another row. This time I would work on a particular aspect of my stroke over a longer distance than in the morning. We typically stuck to the routine of working on strength and speed in the morning and endurance in the afternoon.

In the single scull, efficiency is a must. In the afternoon I would work on improving my aerobic capacity through steadily maintained exertion. Usually there was no coach looking over my shoulder. I had to use my familiarity with the flaws of my stroke to select the drills that would help me remedy those flaws. Trying to remain aware of my mistakes at all moments proved challenging while training alone. Implementing the appropriate solutions and maintaining my target heart rate for aerobic work was even harder. An acquaintance once joked to me that the difference between an elite sculler and an intermediate sculler is that the elite sculler keeps making the same mistakes over and over again. Top-notch scullers must be able to determine what is broken and find a way to fix it.

By the time our afternoon row concluded I had been on the water for two and a half to three hours that day. Sometimes we maintained this schedule for six days of the week. Occasionally, when the weather was too much of an impediment to row on the water, we stayed inside and worked on the ergometer in the gym. These workouts were tedious and monotonous. They did not afford the thrill of being in a boat gliding over water. Balance was not a factor; there were no spectacular views; there were no oars to feather and catch in the water. The ergometer reduced the sport to its most basic cardiovascular benefits. It is one thing to row outside on the water for three hours, it is quite another to row indoors looking at a wall that stands a few feet ahead. Still, the ergometer was a necessary instrument in our workout routine. It offered the chance to gauge stroke ratings, speeds and fitness levels in a more controlled atmosphere. As I had learned in my training in Augusta under Igor Grinko a few years before, if I wanted to be a great sculler, I would have to accept the ergometer as an important aspect of the sport. So, our training for the Olympic Trials often involved time on the ergometer even if the weather outside shone gloriously. Erg or no erg, by the time I left the boathouse in the evening, exhaustion ruled my body. It was time to go home and relax at the Aquinas with Father Tom and the rest of my teammates.

I used to wonder why priests were called "Father," but after living at the Aquinas Institute with FT, I had a much better idea. Spirituality has always played an important role in my life, and I imagine that has something to do with why I was drawn to the Aquinas and to FT. Growing up, my father was a Moslem and my mother was a Catholic. The different religious affiliations present in my home life were not so much a conflict, however, as much as they were an opportunity to experience a variety of cultural and spiritual backgrounds. Both my parents drew from their respective religions the moral lessons they needed to raise me. As I aged and began to question my views on spirituality, religion and my purpose for being alive, I found that Catholicism was the religious framework that suited me best. In many ways, the religion chose me. That spring I underwent the Rites of Christian Initiation. If my beliefs do not adhere strictly to the scriptures or the doctrines endorsed by the church, I at least try to maintain a steadfast belief in God, and I do my best to sustain an appreciation of the glory and spiritual value God has given the world.

There was a time I remember during my training when I had lapsed in my commitment to my family. I neglected to communicate as frequently as I should with the ones I love, and I was not fulfilling the duties my mother believed me to have owed the family. I recall writing her a letter then in which I explained to her some of the feelings that I experienced at that station in my life. It was important for me to explain to her that, lately, when I was so immersed in training for the Olympic Trials, my focus had been narrow and devoted. I often felt alone. In the letter, I apologized if she felt I had neglected the family, but I conveyed that in those days I steered clear of everyone. All I had was rowing and God. I was not depressed or even lonely, because I made the rounds socially when I could and rather enjoyed the constant company of similar minded peers. Instead, what I meant to tell my mother was the entire devotion I had to being the best I could be and to pursuing my greatest dream of making the Olympics. In a way, rowing and God were the only two constants in my life on a day-to-day level. I know that when my rowing career is over, God will still remain as a guide to see me through the difficult times we all experience at different points in our lives.

It was an amazing opportunity I had in Princeton in the months prior to the Olympic Trials. Not only was I in a religious atmosphere that helped focus my training and remind me of my higher purpose, but the everyday benefits of the opportunities in Princeton were a privilege that I could never overlook. It is easy to put training in a vacuum and imagine that the only difficulty in preparing for the Olympics is constantly training hard. What often goes unnoticed, though, is that when one loves a sport and has a complete commitment to it, the physical training is itself more enjoyable than it is a nuisance. The largest difficulties come from practical concerns like earning a living and finding a schedule open enough to accommodate the demands of full-time rowing. In many ways, a rower's life is like an artist's. It may take hard work to create great art, but the numerous hours spent trying are not the difficulty. The struggle is making enough income to sustain the commitment to creating the art. We weren't starving artists; we were starving rowers.

This is why I enjoy taking a moment to appreciate all the opportunity that my experience training in Princeton has afforded. Rowing may be a sport traditionally seen as being for the elite, Ivy League, wealthy types who presumably have the luxury to devote their time to whatever interests or hobbies they choose. The Princeton area has something of that reputation about it. I can hardly dispute the truth behind the sport's historically white and wealthy participants. But the sport is changing rapidly, and regardless of the perception it may still evoke among the majority of those outside it, rowing attracts people from all walks of life. For someone like me, who is not the stereotypical rower, my blessings have been great. Sometimes all the water just flattens in front of you and your path is clear and unobstructed. In Princeton, my waters cleared and calmed. My job gave me freedom, challenging work and money. My home gave me a place to sleep and a spiritual balance that were much needed in a time when rowing was the heaviest weight on the scales of my life. And naturally, the Princeton Training Center gave me a chance to work toward my dreams with a great coach and with friends who I will have for the remainder of my years. I believe people should take a moment every day to appreciate the advantages they have and the good opportunities they have been given, even when it seems their life is an uphill struggle. My struggle to make the Olympic Team was indeed a distant and trying challenge, but I did have a lot in my favor, and it sustained me to take constant notice of my privileges.

Meanwhile, I continued to train. Every day approaching the Trials, my mind became more focused on the task at hand. I thought of rowing when I woke up in the morning. It filled my thoughts at work. I spoke of it at dinner. I dreamt of it while sleeping. Like no other time of my life, I entered the "crew world" in which every part of my life became an extension of my involvement in rowing. The sport was so much a part of who I was that I could no longer separate myself from my existence as a sculler. Since my event is the single scull, it demands that I be in touch with myself in a way other rowers who sweep or scull in team boats do not require. Whether working with a team or independently, I could only attribute my success or failure to my own performance and effort. While at George Washington, where I rowed in the eight, I experienced the reliance team players place on the members of their team. Very few thrills can surpass the sensation achieved when rowing in unison with seven other rowers and a coxswain, each of whom is trying equally as hard, and all of whom function at precisely the same level of mental and physical effort. If there is one sensation in rowing that does beat it, I believe the single scull offers that feeling.

In the single, I am my only competitor. Like I told my mother in my letter, out on the water in that boat, it's just me. I find rowing remarkable for its magical ability to become a personified friend of sorts. Though I may be alone out there on the water, I also have the sport by my side. When one places oneself in the "crew world" or in any lifestyle centered on a particular practice, that practice becomes a companion. Like the puddles from my oars that ripple in circles then fade into the water that made them, rowing made its mark, then melted into an inextricable part of my life.

By late summer I felt more ready for the Olympic Trials than I had felt for any of the National Team Trials of years before. It was a nice reward to look at my past few years in the sport and honestly be able to say that I improved each year. But those consolations were becoming tiresome to me. In 2000 I wanted to make the Olympic Team with a zeal that words, in their weakness, would only betray. Nothing would stand in my way.

At least, nothing would stand in my way until two weeks before the Trials, when Don Smith decided to compete in the single scull event. Don, who placed fifth in the 1996 Olympics while rowing for the United States in the eight, made a surprising decision to go for the single at the 2000 Olympic Trials. I had known all year that it was possible that either Cyrus, Jamie, or Don could make a last minute decision to row in the single instead of a multi-seated boat, but I had hoped to have enough time to prepare if any such challenge became a reality. When Don moved to the single, I did not understand the logic behind his choice. It offended me somewhat that he thought he could just come to the Trials in the single and walk away with my spot on the team. I wasn't scared to race Don. No, I welcomed the opportunity because I knew that Don was fast in the single. The only other time that I had raced him in anything other than a practice was at the Speed Order race in 1999, and I had won there. I knew that if I beat him in the Trials then no one could rightfully say that I only became an Olympian because there was no one to race me. In other words, with Don in the race, the Trials for the single scull suddenly became a tough and legitimate contest. Don had won the 1999 Head of the Charles Regatta in the single, albeit at a three mile distance. The Olympic Trials course would be shorter than the Head of the Charles, but he was an elite rower with every chance to win the event and prevent me from reaching my goal.

When the Singles Trials began in Camden, NJ, Don and I were the top seeded scullers. There were 33 entries in the single, making it the largest event in the regatta. The only other sculler who I believed had a chance at winning was Steve Gillespie, from Augusta. The high amount of participants meant that there would be a time trial on Wednesday night, June 7, to reduce the field to the most competitive of the bunch. Like the National Trials of the year before, my top competitors would be my friends. Throughout my years in rowing, I had come to know Don fairly well. He trained with me at Princeton Training Center leading up to the race, and our mutual training regimen formed a bond between us that many rowers share. In the days preceding the Trials, I sparred with Don a couple of times in mock races on Lake Carnegie. Training with Don most of the year would make our final races even more intense, especially since the format of the regatta was such that the winner would have to win a best out of three series at the end of the week long events. This format for the single event was not particularly unusual, but it certainly made strategy important.

Strategy came into play when determining how much to exert myself in any one race. There could be eight races before winning the event by the end of the week, and every bit of energy I could save might make a difference. To some degree, there was a value in saving energy for the more important races after the time trial. But then I thought, *the Olympic Trials that I've been aiming for my entire rowing career are no place to start loafing.* It was crucial to perform well in Wednesday's time trial because the results determined the order of the heats that would be raced on Thursday.

In Wednesday's time trials, we raced alone against the clock over a 2000 meter course. Each sculler alternated lanes and started on 30-second intervals. With only time to compete against, enacting the best strategy was a tricky challenge. Those who had less experience than I did in the single probably faced the biggest difficulty. They were likely accustomed to the timing and rhythm of working with a team and rowing alongside competing boats. My training had been different, because it had been primarily solitary. I knew the feeling of sculling alone and relying on my own inner clock to ensure I kept the pace needed to achieve the necessary time. While others may have found it difficult to row alone without teammates and without competitors to gauge their performance, those were the aspects of the single I liked the best. Though I knew the value of pacing myself, I decided to take the approach I believe to be best in all aspects of life. If I were to make a mistake, I figured it would be better to err on the side of giving too much and trying too hard, rather than give too little and pay the consequences.

On Wednesday afternoon I finished first among the field at the time trials, crossing the finish line with a time of 6:47.6. A light and quartering tail wind blew to our advantage, and my time had a three second cushion over the next closest sculler. Steve Gillespie, who trained in Augusta with Igor, finished second, and Don Smith came in third. Both were three and four seconds behind me, respectively. Jim Neil, who converted to the single from a larger boat for the Trials, and who had trained with me at the Princeton Training Center, finished fifth. In front of him was a lightweight sweep convert named Erik Miller. Erik was my roommate at the Aquinas. These five people would be the top contenders in the days that followed. The lower half of the field had been eliminated in a matter of minutes, and now it was just the best sixteen that remained. Finishing first gave me confidence that I could produce the type of speed necessary to win a berth on the Olympic team. That first race was one of the most nerve-wracking races I have ever been in, but it eliminated all jitters and helped me get on track.

Before ultimate victory could arrive, I would have to get through Thursday. Winning on Wednesday qualified me to compete in an easier heat on Thursday morning. I would race against Tim Peterson, Gerard Sweeney and Timothy Whitney, who had finished eighth in the time trials the day before. If I won my morning heat, I would skip the repecharge that afternoon and advance directly to Friday's semi-final.

The crowd on Thursday bustled along the shores of the Cooper River. Whereas Wednesday's trial had been relatively calm, on Thursday the general ambiance of the regatta took form in high fashion. This may not have been as glamorous a regatta as the Henley Royal Regatta, but the Olympic Trials had a unique feeling that was no less spectacular. Only at the Olympic Trials would four years of effort and hard work come to a culmination. I could think of no other place that I would rather have been.

The conditions were good. A slight tail wind covered the river, suiting me fine. The Camden course was known for being a fast course, and I had no problem with that because the sooner the race was over the closer I would be to my goal. I rowed down to the starting line and went through my race day warm up. I locked into the start and adjusted my point. The official gave the starting sign and I flew off the line. By the 750 meter mark I had enough of a lead so that I was able to shift my rating down and watch as my competitors raced for second place. With the help of the crowd, I became inspired for the Olympics that were now just three months away. The supporters cheering from the shore and the reporters loitering around the boat enclosure excited me; they renewed the energy I'd spent in

Wednesday's trial, and I went on to win my heat convincingly.

As I expected, everyone who was favored to win the single on Thursday had little problem doing so. My victory was never in doubt and I finished the race with a rating of 31 strokes per minute. The other races were not close either. Don Smith's win was secured when he pulled ahead 100 meters into the race. Steve Gillespie won by two lengths, and Jim Neil had the closest race but pulled out ahead as expected. Friday would be the true day we tested ourselves, and that race would be much closer.

After my race Thursday morning, I spent the remainder of the day relaxing and trying to envision my upcoming races. As the championship race slowly approached, my focus grew more refined. Those early mornings on the water, those nights talking with Father Tom and the rest of the guys, those hours inside on rainy days riding the ergometer — all these experiences seemed to funnel into the Olympic Trials. Now the walls of the funnel drew tighter and tighter as the Trials neared their completion.

On Friday morning I felt the closeness of my goals like objects I could touch. My confidence remained positive and my focus resolute. Now the strategy of the race would change. There would no longer be any room to save energy. I could either give everything I possibly had to give, or I would walk away from these Trials empty handed like I had in the World Championship Trials for the last four consecutive years. Remembering the defeat and agony I felt when losing before, I had more determination to succeed than I had in the past. I also had the confidence. Not only did I know my skill level was high enough to make the Olympic Team, others believed so as well. No longer was I an underdog. This would be my year.

In the semi-final I had to race against Steve Gillespie. He was pretty much an unknown factor at the time. I hadn't raced him in over a year, and all reports from Augusta claimed that Steve was fast. I knew that I had to win the semi-final race convincingly to put any doubts that I had to rest. That morning I burst from the starting line with the speed and power of someone incapable of being restrained. I allowed for no hesitation in my charge, and I drew up my intensity to a passionate, emotional level. Each stroke drove me a little further than the stroke before. While others may have saved a little for the finals, I wanted to come out on Friday with a solid effort and secure my place in Saturday's first final event. By race's end, I had finished first. I was ready to continue the next day with another equally as dominant performance.

Ah, Saturday at last — the first day of the final rounds! There is great relief felt in advancing through the preliminary phases of an event and finally reaching the last steps. All the jitters, the excessive need for strategy, the pressure to make a good showing, all of it disappeared with the finals. By making it to Saturday's race, I had established a firm footing among my other competitors and placed myself in prime position to reach my intended destination. But Sydney was still three months away, and more immediately I would have to pass three intense days before a spot on the Olympic Team could even be anything near a reality. Those three days, I thought, would be strenuous, no doubt, but not impossible. On Saturday I felt better than I had on the days before. I seemed to have paced myself perfectly; I was ready to reach my peak at the precise moment when I needed it to secure victory.

As often happens when in a groove or on a hot streak, my confidence carried over to my physical performance. I looked back over the last several years training to earn a place on the U.S. National Sculling Team, and I could see clearly how much I had grown. My posture was straight and certain. My strokes were stronger and more efficient than they had ever been. All those characteristics that signify a mature rower and a more developed person had grown upon me, and in the 2000 Olympic Trials they appeared, as I had never noticed them previously.

It is difficult to explain the sensation I mean to convey, because these moments of self-recognition are so rare and precious in life that each person experiences them uniquely. For me, the experience was much like looking in a mirror and recognizing, if only for a moment, the Aquil Abdullah that is seen by other people. Or, the experience resembled hearing a recording of my own voice and perceiving how others hear me speak. By Saturday, I had made an enormous step in my development as a person, and that is my ultimate goal. I felt as though I had finally committed to something and that I was finally going to get what I deserved. I looked at myself through objective eyes and saw the confident, mature and fully capable rower I had always wanted to become. Taking a step away from the Trials on Saturday, and moving away from myself even, gave me an edge I felt I had not had in the past. It was the sort of advantage one cannot restrict to statistics or quantifiable explanations. Rather, I gained the awareness that no matter how alone I ever felt out there on the water, no matter how reliant I was on no one but myself, that freedom of independence — to make my own decisions, to pursue my own dreams, to write my own destiny — that freedom was what made all people of the earth such amazing, wonderful and capable human beings. As I sat in my boat on the water of the Cooper River, a slight tail wind carried over the surface against my skin, and it shook me from these thoughts. When I came to, I had easily won the first of potentially three finals.

The victory on Saturday gave me an enormous advantage. In order to win the Trials and make the U.S. Olympic Sculling Team, someone had to win two out of three final races. Having won the first day, all I had to do was win on Sunday and I would be packing a suitcase for Sydney. The dynamics of competition change considerably when one approaches so near to one's goals. There I was only one race away, probably less than a seven minute sprint from making the Olympic Team, and I had breezed through to that point with relative ease. Of course, it felt easy once I had arrived, because the work to reach that point was already behind me. In reality, making my way to where I had arrived was a tough and demanding path. Perhaps I forgot some of the work involved. Maybe I caught a glimpse of victory and allowed myself to lapse on Sunday when I could have secured my win. It could be that somewhere in the corner of my mind, I was so confident in my ability based on the last several races that I didn't exert as much energy as I should have. Maybe I had just become too comfortable. Nevertheless, no mental lapse or physical problem can explain why I lost on Sunday. Although I tried my best, on Sunday, in the second final, I gave a pathetic performance.

There were four scullers competing in the finals. On Saturday, Don finished second behind me, and Steve finished third. Their times were, respectively, around 2 and 8 seconds slower than mine. On Sunday, the results differed considerably. When the Sunday race began, among humid and hazy conditions, I quickly jumped out to an early lead. For the first 1000 meters, my wind felt strong and I maintained a short advantage on Don. But then, about halfway through the race, my stroke rate dropped and my breath let up. Don pulled ahead and I slowed down. He won by almost four seconds. I still managed to finish second ahead of Steve, but Don's victory made a six second turnaround from the day before. My performance was poor and inadequate. It was one of those days when things just don't click. I began to wonder: *Had I reached my peak on Saturday and dropped off on Sunday?* Perhaps I had. Perhaps I had given all there was left in me to give, and, halfway to the finish line, I could no longer muster more energy to emerge ahead. If this were the case, I was finished. Don seemed to be ascending to his peak right as I descended from mine. My only hope was the third and deciding finals race scheduled the next day, Monday morning. This time it would just be Don, and me, but did I have the energy to pick myself up and win?

Prior to the Olympic Trials, while training in Princeton, I set time goals for myself in order to reach the speed I needed to win the Trials. I calculated that if I were to win the Olympic Trials that year in the single, I would have to row a time of 6:51. That time would have to be much faster to medal at the Olympics, but first I had to make it there. Because I reasonably expected a time of 6:51 to suffice in winning the Trials, I mentally grouped the goal of rowing a 6:51 second race with winning a berth on the U.S. Olympic Sculling Team. In the past I had rowed a 6:47 in a tail wind, so I thought for sure that I should be able to row a time of 6:50 down the Trials' course in flat conditions.

After my exhausting race on Sunday, I spent the remainder of the day resting and relaxing in preparation for Monday's race. I sat in my room, watched TV and ordered room service. I talked to my mother once that day and did nothing else. Like the National Trials in 1999, this would be another instance when I went head to head against a friend. What had I learned in the year since racing against Jamie? Had I really come to terms with losing to someone so evenly matched, who had trained no harder than I had? Would I ever fully come to terms with it? All I knew for sure was the confidence and faith I felt in myself. I may have reached my peak, but I would just have to dig deeper and find some way to do what had to be done. Up against defeat, there was no longer any other choice.

Looking for inspiration, that night I had dinner with my new Godfather, Mike Teti. Earlier in the spring when I underwent the Rites of Christian Initiation I had asked Mike to be my Godfather. Many people have asked me why I chose him to fill that role, and the answer has always been simple. Mike has given me the opportunity to improve myself as an athlete by training in Princeton, and he has allowed me to improve myself as a human being by demanding me to perform at my best. Mike and I had never spent any time alone, and this was the first time that he told me that he thought I could really do it. He told me to put everything out of my mind and focus on racing. He told me that God helps those who help themselves, and that it was now up to me to do what had to be done and that God was there to remind me that I could succeed. After dinner, I remember going back to my hotel room, where I called up my good friends Jeff Hanna and his sister, Tricia, and I told them what time I was racing. The evening paced itself slowly. Ready for the big day, I finally went to bed.

Monday. June 12, 2000. Camden, N.J. The Cooper River. U.S. Olympic Sculling Team Trials, Day Six. Shortly before 8:00 a.m. The last day.

On Monday, the hazy and windy weather of the previous days disappeared to reveal a tranquil, warm and pleasant morning. The Cooper River cast reflections from the trees along the banks, and the winds died down to a calm and still repose. Most of the fans and participants had left on Sunday afternoon. The majority of the crowd throughout the Olympic Trials had been people directly involved in rowing, either as coaches, athletes or sponsors. Many were former rowers who still lived in the Princeton or Philadelphia area. Since the single scull was the only event to reach a third final, all other events had finished on Sunday and most fans left with them. Monday morning, before my 8:00 a.m. race against Don, the grandstands contained only the remaining diehard rowers and scattered family members. Something about that morning will never leave me: the silence. Every person there seemed to make no noise. The bustle of people mingling and catching up on old times had all died by Monday. There remained only a quietude that served to heighten the tension in the air.

Even the water, crystalline and motionless, seemed to hold its breath as I sat in my boat, across from Don, waiting for the race to begin. My mother was in the crowd, as she had been for most of the week, but now I felt her presence like I hadn't in the other races. And while I registered her being there, and while I even registered every coach, friend and peer who sat on the shore watching, I was utterly alone in my boat. All were watching Don and me to see who would represent the United States' single sculling boat in the Sydney Olympics. The race may have meant a lot to those who watched, and it certainly meant a lot to Don and me, but in the greater scheme it would bring little fame and no fortune. I was just another guy trying to do what he does and do it well. With this attitude, I braced myself, summoned all strength, and, when the starting signal sounded, gave my oars a strong clean catch through the water. I was off.

In the opening of the race, I am told, Don and I were even for several strokes. Midway through the course, I slipped ahead to a half-length lead. At the time, I had little conception of who led the battle. My focus turned inward, and I sensed the lead changes as they occurred, but never took much conscious notice of them. All I could do was row my hardest, give my all and hope everything turned out as planned. With about 750 meters remaining, Don drew even. I continued to pull and press, remembering all the advice my coaches had given me in the past. *Out quickly with the hands on the slide! Reach with the hips!* All my coaches watched from the banks as my form approached a perfection it had never known. No one will ever row with *perfect* form for an entire race, but I came as close as I ever had. My catches were pristine and crisp, my distance long, my balance symmetrical and the overall technique sound and finely polished. In the final 500 meters, I nosed ahead. Only a few dozen strokes remained. With every one of those strokes, my goal approached. *6:51. Olympic Team. Slide. Catch. Push with the legs.*

When the course ended and we crossed the line at the finish, neither of us knew who won. Each of us had given his all. Over the 2000 meter course, I never led by more than half the length of a boat. Don never led by more than a few feet. There were so many minuscule lead changes it would be impossible to measure them all. But when the results came in, Don had crossed the line a few inches ahead. Those few inches amounted to a 33 hundredths of a second victory. Don clocked in at 6:50.18, and I finished in 6:50.51. I'd raced the time I set out to race. In fact, I'd slightly *beaten* the time I wanted to race. But it was not enough. I would not be packing for Sydney.

CHAPTER 6

The Pineapple Cup

Looking back on how I felt after racing Don Smith at the 2000 Olympic Rowing Trials almost brings me to tears. I didn't feel like crying when I lost; I was still in a state of shock. I had just raced the most strenuous, and one of the fastest races of my life, and I could only think that Don was one tough man. I had tossed everything at him, and he still didn't cave. It wasn't until I looked at my mother standing on the shores of the Cooper River that my eyes began to swell with tears and my throat began to hurt as I choked back wave after wave of primal screams. Alone was the only thing I wanted to be, alone in my single, alone on the water, as I had been so many mornings on Lake Carnegie. I didn't practice alone, but for some reason I always felt alone. Even with an extended family as big as mine, I felt alone. With the throngs of people giving me support and telling me how proud they were of me, I felt alone. In the arms of a beautiful woman, I felt alone. Even with the encouraging words of my godfather, or with the tears of one of my best friends, who knew the same pain, I felt alone. I felt this way because my defeat was singular. There was only one other person who could possibly understand, and he was the victor of the race. Don crossed the finish line 33 hundredths of a second ahead of me, and for that he had won the right to represent the United States of America in the 2000 Olympic games.

And so, in the wake of my loss, even much later, I reflect on my experience at the Trials. The multitude of emotions is strong. They still choke me up today as I try to make new National Teams however I can. The bottom line is that I felt like a loser. I felt like a wimp and a failure. No matter how many times I was told that I raced an incredible race, I would remain a wimp in my own mind until I redeemed myself. In a way, this book is my redemption. It is my story. This is for all of those who, like myself, have felt alone after defeat.

Where do we go after defeat? What should I do next? What more was there to be done? After finishing that race and realizing I'd lost, I was nonplussed. I learned sometime later that my mother didn't know what to do either. She wanted to console me, but had no idea what words or gestures would convey the strength of emotions needed in such a catastrophic time. She asked Ken Dreyfuss, my coach from the Potomac Boat Club, *"What do I say to him?"* The truth is words and consolation came no easier for me than they did for her. I had given my life to the pursuit of making the Olympic Rowing Team, and now that I failed to reach the goal, it felt in many respects like I had nothing of my life left.

One thing that I failed to look at when I first lost was the fact that I had only really trained hard for two years. It takes eight years to become a doctor, it takes three years to become a lawyer and it takes numerous years to do anything worthwhile. If we look at people who excel in any arena, it is very easy to talk about how much natural talent they have. What we do not see is the countless number of hours they have spent honing the skills they have and gaining the skills that they did not have in order to reach the point where everything they do seems effortless. It would be foolish for me to believe that I could be as good as Tiger Woods in golf or Michael Jordan in basketball, or even Steven Redgrave in rowing. The one thing that I could do was require of myself the same amount of dedication, commitment and effort as those who excel in any area of life.

I tried to remember that talented people work really hard to excel in their area of expertise, but in most cases, they work really hard at everything else too. Michael Jordan is now a successful businessman. Former professional wrestler Jessie "The Body" Ventura is now an elected politician in Minnesota. There are numerous other examples of athletes who are successful outside of their sport. One quality that distinguishes the ordinary from the excellent is a sense of balance found in those who reach the top.

Placing one's entire self into the determined pursuit of a single aim can be a blind and risky business. How do we get to the point where we place all of our self worth in one thing? How do we become blind? I had always believed single-minded determination was necessary in the pursuit of excellence, whether in sports or in any other aspect of life, but now my perspective has changed. We need balance. Great value can be found in devoting oneself to a specific purpose, and much can be gained through the pursuit of that aim. Anyone who wants and attempts to master a certain skill or to reach a high level of excellence in a given field deserves commendation. Excellence and mastery do not come easily for anyone, no matter how much natural talent a person possesses. While I cannot condemn working hard for a single goal, losing in the Olympic Trials against Don really made me realize the importance of living a life with balanced passions and pursuits. A balanced life makes for well-rounded, fascinating human beings.

Some sports require athletes to train six hours a day and some sports do not allow the athlete to focus on anything other than the sport for long periods of time. Although the training for rowing is intense, it allows oarsmen the chance to engage in other endeavors. Consider the distinguished careers of athletes like Steven Redgrave, Bob Kahler and Jeff Klepacki. Each has managed to build a successful rowing career *and* a successful business career. In my life, at least since 1998, rowing has taken precedence above all other interests. Nevertheless, I shudder to think what a limited person I would be, if, given my love of the saxophone and my success in the work place, I let these interests slip away from the wholeness of my personality.

The subject I presently address is tricky territory, because I understand the importance of being excellent at something, and I also understand — all too well — how hard one has to work to reach that level of excellence. The Olympic Trials taught me a valuable lesson about balancing my life. I would shudder to see that lesson mistaken as a suggested path of diverse mediocrity. Finding reconciliation between the single-minded dedication required of excellence and the benefits of embracing a variety of interests can be a difficult task. Perhaps the best way to do so is to examine why we undertake an endeavor in the first place. What do we seek to gain from those activities we choose to occupy our lives?

In the case of sports, I believe all athletes participate in sports because, to varying degrees, they value the combination of a physical and mental challenge that sports provide. Measuring ourselves physically and mentally against others who attempt to do the same is rewarding insofar as the competition involved in taking these measurements helps build physical prowess, mental toughness and ideally, a stronger character. Outside of sports, what reasons do we have for undertaking an endeavor? At the most fundamental level, we probably choose to do what we do because in some sense we stand to gain from that decision. Whether that means taking a prestigious job to earn money, playing music to tap into the soul or drinking booze because it makes you feel good, most things we do are done because they give us some sort of benefit. Given the infinite number of courses we can choose for our lives, great argument can surround which activities and undertakings are more productive, useful or healthy than others. In some cases, as with illegal drugs, for example, society on a whole would probably agree that there are more meaningful and healthy ways to live. Everyone must choose his or her own path, and although some paths may be widely recognized as better or worse than others, ultimately, the only right path for each person is the one he or she actively and independently chooses.

It seems to me, what we make of our resources and what we do with our time determines how successful we are as people. I may never be a superb saxophonist, but I can be a superb rower and a good saxophonist if I structure my time right. Likewise, I may never be a superb businessman, but I can be a superb rower and a good businessman. For some people, pursuing one end to the point of excellence may be the best decision. For others, sampling from a more diverse plate of interests may be more appropriate. Diversity allows one to appreciate what is truly important in one's life. I don't think that I ever have been or ever will be the type of person capable of pursuing a single goal while totally ignoring every other aspect of my life. I have learned to be the type of person who structures his time wisely and gets the most out of every opportunity.

Finding a balanced life is tough for people who strive to be the best at what they do. In sports, our society places a high premium on being the one to stand on the highest medal platform. From being the best we gain accolades from friends and family, fame from adoring fans, a validation of who we are and what we do. Very easily, the pursuit of the gold becomes a pursuit of ourselves; we believe that the glory defines who we are. So what happens when we don't win the gold? If we are to maintain our self-esteem, we must change how we define who we are. In the pursuit of excellence, we can easily arrive at a narrow measurement of our worth, and this happens in all aspects of life. No matter what we do, our society gives great importance to trophies, medals, icons and awards because they symbolize the excellence that we strive to achieve. Although these symbols are useful as visible and tangible emblems of success, I believe it is valuable to remember that they are merely symbols. The gold medal is just a symbol of my love for my sport; it is a symbol of my commitment, a symbol of my determination, a symbol of my desire to win. But in the end it is merely a symbol that says I was the best on one day at one moment in time. It says nothing about what I will be or do for the rest of my life. Far more important is the work and love involved in obtaining it. Every time we train, our training is another symbol indicating our love for our sport. Intense training can often lead to an unbalanced and single-minded life. Whether or not this is best for any given person I cannot say. Most important is what we gain through our training. As I can personally attest, not everyone comes home with the gold. Those who do are winners, without doubt, but they are not the only ones who emerge from their efforts with something gained.

What have I won by not winning the Olympic Trials? The question is actually very shallow, because it only looks at one event in the past three years. I think the better question asks, "What have I gained from training to be an Olympic caliber sculler?" That question is more relevant, and easier to answer. It is a question that I believe all athletes who attempt to achieve Olympic glory should ask of themselves. If your goal is to achieve something different than the Olympics, be it a strong relationship, a closeness to God, a promotion at work, a mastery of Scrabble, whatever it happens to be, you ought always to ask yourself what you have gained from trying to reach your goals.

It's easy to say what you win if you attain your goals. If you achieve Olympic glory, you can say, "I have a gold medal," or, "I have done something that has never been done before." But those who don't actually make it to the Olympics and those who don't make the medal stands may have a harder time determining what they have gained from all their training. In the end, we must remember the age old wisdom that no matter what the goal, those who try persistently and rigorously to achieve something always gain a lot from trying. The challenge — particularly when one falls short of his or her objective — is to have a perspective that will enable one to see all he or she has gained in the process, and to correct those decisions that deterred the achievement of the goal in the first place. This can be difficult when one fixes so resolutely on a single aim and operates with a mentality that suggests anything shy of that aim is a failure. In my case, once I saw through that narrow focus, I realized that what I have gained has enriched my life and made me an immensely better person. I can say that I am in the best shape of my life. I can say that I am one of the best scullers in the United States, that I have met some of the greatest human beings in the world, that the support shown to me by friends and family through my training shows me how much I am loved. I can say that I was part of one of the greatest dual races in American history, and I can say that on one day in my life, I gave my best. I could go on listing what I have gained, but the important fact is my life has been enriched so much as a result of training to be an Olympic caliber sculler. Achieving my goal of becoming an Olympian was merely the carrot that helped me along the path to becoming a better person. And although I would obviously have preferred to win that race against Don and reach my actual goal, what I did win is a greater understanding of why I do what I do, and how I can work more wisely to achieve other goals in my life.

If we take enough time to look at our lives and ask what we gain in pursuit of something, we will all become better, more honest people and thus do our part in making a positive contribution to society. Those who we label as winners get the momentary recognition of being the best, and being the best is one of the few differences between first place, second place, third, fourth and all the others who finish below the top. When the challenge is over, though, only one person can reach that top level. Don and I raced incredible races at the 2000 Olympic Trials. Reporters likened it to a prizefight bout between two evenly matched boxers. But the course ended when it did, and at that time, Don was ahead. Someone always has to win in racing sports, and because someone always has to win, someone else always has to lose. In 2000, I was that loser. Did that make me unsuccessful? I don't think so.

I have spent many hours wondering what it means to be successful. Is our success in sport defined solely by the results of a race, or is it measured by how much we improve from where we started? In the Olympic Trials I had a personal goal to row 6:51. I beat my goal, yet it was not enough. Were my efforts a success since I accomplished my performance goal? I'd set a target and hit it as planned. *Of course I was a success*, I thought. Then I realized: *No I wasn't. I lost.* When I thought some more I discovered what seems to me the best explanation of success. I believe that success in life is determined by the extent to which we use our experiences, both good and bad, to learn the lessons that make us better people. True winners rebound after a tragic experience. Although more people fail to reach the top than those who succeed, we can all be winners if we make a concerted effort to learn from every experience in our lives. Unfortunately, this is easier in theory than in practice. In reality, profound emotions are involved. It hurts bitterly to try your hardest and still not finish first. What do we learn as athletes, as human beings, when we are not first? The answer depends on how much we try to learn. Certainly if we seek to turn a sour outcome into a positive experience, we will head in the right direction. But so often in sports, work or other parts of our lives, we forget why we started an endeavor. Finding a positive outcome from a seemingly negative experience then seems impossible.

As I mentioned before, we often choose to undertake the various activities in our lives because we stand to benefit from them in some fundamental way. Enjoyment alone proves this point. For instance, when a child first kicks a soccer ball, she does so because it's fun. Next, the child wants to score a goal. After the child scores her first goal, she wants to score another, because it felt good to accomplish something. Only after this, when other people want to score goals too, does the thought of winning become an issue. It may take longer, but the child starts to hone her skills in order to improve, to play like Mia Hamm. Eventually, perhaps, the child grows into a woman who plays soccer passionately and holds the sport as an inextricable part of her existence. In the more veteran stages of participation in a sport, that original joy at kicking the ball becomes clouded by all the other dynamics involved in being a high caliber athlete. If we take a moment to remember the original and most fundamental reasons we do what we do, I would imagine that nine times in ten, we will realize that — win or lose — we've had what we wanted all along. This is not to suggest we shouldn't keep score in sports, because keeping score helps us measure our own improvement. Rather, people should always try to remember the original reasons why they began participating in any endeavor, regardless of the scores they earn along the way.

Now, as I reflect on why I began rowing, I would like to introduce the idea of the Pineapple Cup. The Pineapple Cup is the prize given to the winner of the Diamond Challenge Sculls at the Henley Royal Regatta. Here I use the term "Pineapple Cup" as a metaphor for those important goals we all have in our lives. For me, it was becoming an Olympic caliber sculler and making the Olympic Team in 2000. For others, the Pineapple Cup may be to become president of a company, to make the varsity basketball team as a sophomore in high school or to be elected as a congressman. Everyone's Pineapple Cup signifies some different objective, but we all have a Pineapple Cup for which we strive. Regardless of how important (or unimportant) achieving an objective might be for each individual person, I believe we all covet positive reinforcement from the people around us. There aren't many cheers for the losers. The desire to be applauded and well received can, as I have learned from my personal experience, lead people to define their self worth by their capacity to achieve the Pineapple Cup. If I place my entire self worth on achieving that goal, what does it say about me that I failed to do so? Does it say I am worthless? Of course not! Rather, it simply says that I cannot achieve the Pineapple Cup. It does not mean I cannot achieve different goals, and equally challenging ones at that. The problem, though, is standing up after you've been knocked down.

Looking back on my rowing career, I shudder at the fondness of my memories. I am still young, so my nostalgia may seem premature. The point, I suppose, is that I will never "get over" losing the Olympic Trials in 2000, but I will move past it. That loss, under those circumstances, will always be a source of ire for me, as long as I live. But I have learned not to wallow in my disappointment or in what might easily be perceived as a failure. By not making the 2000 U.S. Olympic Sculling Team, I gained a better understanding of who I am, and a better perspective on the roles my various interests play in my life. It occurred to me, given some time to reflect, that growing as people is the most important victory we can ever achieve in our lives. I have found that one of the hardest things for me to do is to change negative patterns in my life. I have also found that once I have changed those patterns everything else becomes much easier. If I can go through every experience life hands me and use it to learn something that improves me as a person — something that makes me more pleasant to be around, more of a positive influence on the world, more of a role model — then I will always be a winner. This is the validation I have discovered for the work I have put into an endeavor that otherwise may seem to have ended empty handed.

CHAPTER 7

Redemption Row

M any times in my life I have stood one footstep away from achieving my goals. Sometimes, I have taken that step with no impediments and gone on to accomplish all that I thought I could. Other times, I have fallen and been unable to take that last step, leaving me inches from final success. One thing that I have learned through both victory and defeat is that nothing is forever, and as long as one keeps on trying, there will always be another opportunity to succeed.

After the 2000 Olympic Trials, I had some very serious evaluating to do. Coming to terms with my loss at the 2000 Olympic Trials is a process that continues to this day. More immediately, following the race I had to determine what I would do with my rowing career. Although I hadn't won, my performance was still highly commendable. My times had proven that I could compete at an international level. But did I want to get up and try again?

After the interviews were completed, and after my boat was disassembled, I walked over to my mom and she gave me hug. I didn't want to do anything but go back to my hotel room and go to sleep for a long time. During the Trials I had been riding my bike back and forth to the course, but after such an exhausting race I could barely take five steps before I felt like sitting down. The shores of the Cooper River were silent except for the occasional sounds of workmen breaking down the race tents. I saw a close friend named Tricia Hanna, and she came over to console me, but what could she say that hadn't already been said? What could she do that hadn't already been done?

I smiled and asked her for a ride back to my hotel. She agreed, and I told my mother that I would meet her at the hotel for lunch after I had loaded my boat on my jeep.

The ride to the hotel was pretty quiet except for the occasional joke that Tricia told to try to cheer me up. These jokes gave me no solace, as genuine as they were. When we arrived at the hotel, Tricia got out of her car and gave me a hug before continuing on her way. I went up to my room, unlocked the door and closed it firmly behind me. I was finally alone.

On the edge of the bed I sat down, turned on the television and flipped through the channels. Nothing on television could make me forget the disappointment that I felt for failing to achieve my long-standing goal. I turned off the television, packed my bag, checked out of the hotel and went to meet my mother at the Diamond Diner for lunch. There are few moments in my life about which I can recall all the details, but I remember every second of the day I lost the Olympic Trials.

At lunch my mother asked me what I was going to do now that the Trials were over. I told her that there was an outside shot that I could still make the team and go to the Olympics, but that I wasn't really all that hopeful. She said that I should take a small break and do something fun, so I mentioned that I was thinking about going to New York for a couple of days. She thought that was a good idea. After eating, we boarded our separate cars; she headed south to Washington, I headed north back to Princeton.

Once in Princeton, I dropped off my boat and went straight for the Aquinas to pack my bag for New York City. I was determined to forget all about rowing. The drive to New York did not take long because I made it as quickly as I could. When I arrived, I called up some friends so we could hit the town. A few minutes later I had already downed a few drinks at the nearest bar. So began a bender that would culminate a night later when, standing drunk in Times Square howling at the skyscrapers and trying to hail a cab, my cell phone rang.

"Hell-ooo," I said.

"Hello, Aquil? This is your mother." *Uh-oh*, I thought, *time to sober up*. "What are you doing? Where are you?"

"I'm in Times Square, and I'm headed to Ruby Foos to eat some sushi and drink some drinks."

"Well Mike Porterfield has been calling all day trying to find you. He wants to know if you want to row at the Henley."

It was at that moment when I remembered: I am a rower. I had just lost the Olympic Trials by .33 seconds. What am I doing now? The realization stung.

"Okay," I said. "I'll give him a call." I hung up the phone and there I was, standing on a corner in Times Square looking up at the bright lights, completely lost. I was not geographically lost, for I knew right where I was in relation to where I had to be that night. But where was I inside? Where was I going with my life? The truth is, I had no idea.

So I thought about it. I was in the best shape of my life; I didn't have any more races for the summer; I had still had a fairly successful year. Why *not* take a trip to Henley? A large part of me wanted nothing to do with it. After losing to Don in such a physically and emotionally exhausting race, I lacked the energy and enthusiasm to go off and try myself in another highly competitive event. The loss to Don sapped me of my momentum and gave rise to doubts about my involvement in the sport. Had my time training been wasted time? Should I even go on rowing? Although I have since come to terms with these questions, at the time, their answers were not so obvious. If I were to compete in the Henley Royal Regatta it would mean risking defeat again. Not only was my recent loss at the 2000 Olympic Trials a negative influence, but my lingering failure from the mishap with my foot-stretcher at the previous year's Henley also remained with me.

Perhaps because I was already in great shape, maybe because I found it easy to stay within the routine of competitive rowing that I had made of my life, probably also because I believe that the times I am stuck the lowest are the same times I should try to reach the highest, one way or another, I decided to accept the invitation. After several minutes of leaning against a pole in the middle of Times Square, I called Mike Porterfield, and he told me to return to Princeton as soon as possible. I would row in the 2000 Henley.

With the decision to row at the Henley came a lot of concerns, many personal, others practical. I have, in the recent years of my rowing career, been fortunate enough to have benefactors and sponsors such as the National Rowing Foundation, Team Potomac 2000 and Knickerbocker, to help me fund trips both in the U.S. and abroad. So, while there were certainly some practical matters to deal with relating to taking time off from work and arranging to travel overseas, my attitude and outlook were larger issues than the practical ones. Inside I was still a mess. If I were to row at the Henley, I would have to get rid of my overwhelming sense of self-pity and doubt. I would have to move on.

The difficulty was, I didn't quite know how or in which direction to move. All I had was the knowledge that somehow I needed to find the mental edge that I lacked in previous races. I believe that no matter what we do in life, having a mental edge can be an advantage that makes the final difference in determining who comes out ahead of the rest. If we look at team sports, each team usually has a member who they look to when everything is falling apart. Usually this is the guy who never doubts his ability, no matter what the circumstances. Having a mental edge is a complicated ambition, particularly in athletics when so much emphasis depends on one's physical shape and talent. But I believe every physical drill and training effort should be used to build a pattern of thought that leads one to believe that, "no matter what happens, I am prepared."

Mental toughness is an aspect of sports that many top athletes enjoy. No matter how much physical skill one possesses, no one will ever cultivate that skill to its full extent if not pairing it with a confidence of demeanor and a sportsmanlike quality of character. Likewise, one may lack the God-given physical ability to perform well in a given task, but incredible mental toughness may carry that athlete farther than anyone ever thought possible. The unique aspect of mental toughness is its ability to compensate for slight inadequacies in actual talent. The old expression, "It's not the size of the dog in the fight, it's the size of the fight in the dog," holds true in all walks of life. I believe the way to mental toughness must necessarily come through a few trials of defeat. Without losing and tasting the bitterness of failure, one cannot fully appreciate how much sweeter it tastes to win. Without losing, one does not realize that winning is something toward which all mental strength must be directed. Those who have lost profoundly acquire through these losses a more comprehensive and personal understanding of what it takes to have a mental advantage over one's opponent. Although I had considered myself strong mentally (even in the Olympic Trials), I knew I still could improve how keenly I approached my sport.

When I arrived at Henley-on-Thames shortly after my failure in Camden, the new mentally stronger Aquil Abdullah was on the scene. It wasn't that I felt I was a great rower, just that after the Olympic Trials I knew that I could push myself to the limit and that I wouldn't die. I knew that I could push my body to its physical limits and that it would hurt, certainly, but it would only be temporary.

Thus, with a refreshing new outlook, my second trip to Henley-on-Thames began.

The greatest part about rowing all over the world is the friends one makes along the way. When I arrived in London, Rachel Haining, who was kind enough to drive me from the airport to Henley-on-Thames, met me immediately. Rachel is the wife of sculling legend Peter Haining. Peter has competed at the top-level of rowing for many years and dominated in the lightweight single from 1993-1995, winning three gold medals. Rachel and Peter are the driving forces behind the Thames World Sculling Challenge. I met them in 1999 when I raced in the challenge, and we have been friends ever since. When Rachel picked me up the drive was pleasant and she updated me on all of the events in her and Peter's lives. As we drew closer to Henley, I began to admire the English countryside and I started thinking of the racing that would soon follow. It was nice to be back at the Henley.

There are few experiences like rowing at the Royal Henley Regatta, and although I had rowed in the regatta in 1999, when I arrived at Henley-on-Thames for the second time, I was just as amazed at the tradition and regalia as I was the first. Truly, the event is one to behold. I approached the small town that had come to represent such a troubling and unfortunate experience for me, and quickly its charm helped me regain a love of the quaint historical atmosphere that had first enthralled me when I visited the year before. Temple Island stood thick with trees, splitting the Thames in two. Tents and folding chairs bedecked the quiet shores. Down near the water, kids frolicked about, mimicking with their arms the motions of the rowers they saw at eye level on the water. A team of ambulances parked in the car lot of Lion Meadows and waited in case of disaster. An old man who seemed to have been doing this for years, watched attentively, and I heard his walkie-talkie muttering some fuzzy message. Further on, police officers in full uniform directed traffic, traffic that was maddeningly locked in the narrow streets of the nearby town. The police warnings I read about for motorists to mind the changing traffic patterns in the town center made little noticeable change. All bustled. I even heard jazz music playing somewhere in the distance, and though it wasn't the same music I would play on my saxophone, it filled me with inspiration.

When it all began, the banks flushed with the same elegantly dressed fans mingling about with cups of wine and mouths full of shrimp cocktail. A microbrewery had made Hooray Henley beer especially for the regatta, and the richness of the atmosphere seemed greater than I remembered it from the year before. The stewards again hurried around in their navy blazers, making certain that everything ran smoothly. Oarsmen from around the world tended to their boats by adjusting oars, rigging and foot-stretchers. The athletes conversed under the boat tent and around the banks, and they caught up on the latest gossip and news from the sport. From the start I was drawn back in, taken again to that rowing world that had seemed so uncertain after losing in Camden. This was where I belonged, among rowers, among kindhearted people, all seeking the enjoyment and self-improvement to be had through participation in such a singular and endearing sport.

The experience of a single sculler is different from that of those who row in team boats. One of the most challenging differences is that a single sculler must often be his own manager and coach. Usually, I handled most responsibilities involved in participating in a regatta by myself, so it was quite a joy for me to arrive at the Henley in 2000 with a contact at the Leander Club. Thanks to Joe Michaels, a physicist and an outstanding rower who had trained at the Leander Club during his time at Oxford, I was able to obtain permission to lodge my boat at the Leander Club. What I didn't know was that I would have some other people looking after me as well. Jurgen Grobler, the coach of the British straight four, had asked Mark Hatlee to watch after me during my stay in Henley. Mark Hatlee was an invaluable asset, because he handled many of the details about the race that would have been difficult for me to undertake on my own. His assistance also gave me the time to enjoy my visit by mingling with members of the British straight four. Among them was Steven Redgrave, who would become the only endurance athlete to win five gold medals in five consecutive Olympic games. Hanging out with Redgrave and his boat mates Tim Forester, James Cracknell and Matthew Pisent — who were also proven oarsmen — I learned the rules of Cricket and had fun before the time came to focus seriously on my races.

My first race, on the Berks side of the river, pitted me against Simon King from Kingston Rowing Club, London. Unlike the year before, I was completely confident at the start of my first race. Mark, and Boyd from Resolute Racing shells, assured me that if anything were to go wrong with the boat, it would not be the foot-stretchers. For the first time since the Olympic Trials I felt the confidence of a champion. It seemed as though I had regained my mental toughness. This mental toughness of mine was probably unnoticeable by others. Only I could realize the changes I had undergone since the Olympic Trials. Before, my toughness stemmed from a desire to win and a resolute will for success. This sort of mental toughness is important, and I have always been blessed with it in all forms of competition. The toughness I acquired since the Trials, however, was new and from a different source. My new mental strength stemmed from the realization that there is more to life than crew. In the larger scheme of things, I had nothing to lose by competing in the sport. If I lost a race, or even if I lost all my races, there were still other equally important aspects of life to teach me valuable lessons and to improve my character. This new attitude might ostensibly seem to indicate a shift in my values, but rather than let it force me out of competition, I instead chose to let it empower my ability to perform. It was completely compatible with the confidence I had before. In other words, I still wanted to win. I doubt the desire to win and excel will ever leave me, no matter how old I age or how much my skills should deteriorate. My new nothing-to-lose attitude allowed me to compete with an approach that did not fear risking it all for victory. I had already experienced the most devastating defeat imaginable, and now, at the 2000 Henley Royal Regatta, it was time to gain something back.

My race against King went fairly easily. In fact, my race the following day against Giles Monnickendam from Nottinghamshire County Rowing Association went my way convincingly, too. I was ranked number one in the single sculls for the regatta, and my performances in the first two races apparently merited that ranking. The races I remember most vividly are the semi-final and the final. When I look back at these races, the parts I recall most clearly are not the start or the finish, or how great my lead was or how high my stroke rating reached. Instead, I recall the exhilarating feeling that comes when competition reaches its pinnacle. Such a feeling is not backed with specifics, only with a general sense of working incredibly hard and directly challenging someone who is doing the same. When I did some reading from my journals and press clippings to try and recall the details of the race, I came across some live reporting from the Henley 2000, and I think that it conveys the details of the race better than I could probably relay. Here is the verbatim account that was given live from Henley radio during my semi-final race against Colin Greenaway:

> Colin Greenaway successfully defended his Indoor Championship title at the British event last November, but may be no match for Abdullah, a solid international sculler who is trying to fit himself into the U.S. National Team. Off the start, Aquil pretty quick, and two lengths up by the Barrier. Steadily, steadily he slides away and drops the rate, down to 30 by Fawley and three and half lengths ahead of Greenaway. More of the same, coming to Remenham Aquil now down to 28, looking very slick, stable in the boat and comfortable. No stretcher trouble this year, then... Greenaway takes it up past the grandstand, to 35 and counting, but the margin, though narrowing, is not going to affect the outcome. And Abdullah progresses nicely into his final.

Coming across this account now that some time has passed brings me back to the moment in a unique way. Indeed I was a "solid international sculler...trying to fit [my]self into the U.S. National Team." And I took a step in that direction by "progressing nicely" into the final race against Simon Goodbrand, from Britain.

One of the strangest ideas that I have had to deal with in the past couple of years is being considered one of the best. I do not know why, but it is an accolade that I never like to hear. Only now, after having taken some time to reflect on why I row and why I do many of the things that I do, do I fully understand my aversion to the term "one of the best." I want to be one of the best, but I don't want anyone to *expect* me to be one of the best. *Somewhere*, there is always someone better. For me, the idea of playing the underdog will always be more romantic than the idea of playing the champion who always has victory to defend.

The evening after my semi-final I had the pleasure of dining with Don Spero, the last American sculling world champion prior to Jamie Koven, and one of the sport's true gentlemen. Don took me out to dinner with his family. My chaperone of sorts, Mark Hatlee, had given specific instructions that I not drink any beer, but Don looked away as I drank a pint of Guinness. It was good to be surrounded by friends the night before my final race. The feeling of support that I received from the Speros helped me to defeat my aversion toward being "one of the best." At that dinner, I finally knew I was going to be one of the best, and all I had to do was travel the final distance to achieve my goal of winning the Royal Henley Regatta.

In the final, I kept my state of mind focused and relaxed. The challenge ahead lay not in fulfilling the expectations of others, but in fulfilling my expectations for myself. I had a strength that I could only know because I understood the trappings of my own mind and could gauge how my mental perspective had improved from where it had been in the past. The color-commentator who did the live coverage for this race reported:

> Scullers on the start, and they've just started. With the British heavyweight sculler Matthew Wells withdrawn, Abdullah will be hoping for a quiet life, but Goodbrand is going to make life as hard as possible. Level at the end of the island, Abdullah at 38 and Goodbrand a pip higher. Abdullah is on Bucks, Goodbrand on Berks, and at the Barrier it seems to be half a length to the American, who is sculling at 32, Goodbrand at 34, this carries on, but Abdullah starts to steer into the center. He must have been warned, gets back to his station, now 2.5 lengths ahead, but Goodbrand has dropped the rate to 29, and the race looks over. Abdullah stays at 32, Goodbrand at 29, until Remenham, where the American drops a little, and the lead reduces to two lengths. Goodbrand up to 30, Abdullah back to 32 again, the steering is fine, and the lead is still two lengths. Goodbrand bringing it right up for the Enclosures, Abdullah holding him, still two lengths. A spirited 36.5 sprint by the Brit is mashed by Abdullah's 42, and the first black man to win the Diamonds crossed 2/3 length up, time 8:12.

My victory at Henley felt as sweet as my loss in the Trials felt sour. Although making the Olympic Team was my goal, and winning the Henley did not change my exclusion from the team, the win allowed me to let go of my loss at the Trials and move on to the next chapter of my rowing career. It was the sort of victory made significant not only for the prestige and acclaim of its actual award, but for the symbolic ideal the Pineapple Cup represented in my mind. To me, winning the Henley showed me that I could drop as far as possible and still rise to the top. No longer did I need to prove anything to anyone else in the rowing world. I had needed to prove something to myself. Winning the Pineapple Cup at the Henley Royal Regatta gave me the validation I needed to continue in my pursuit of excellence. The questions I had asked after the Olympic Trials now seemed less pressing. The answers were there; I needed only examine and listen.

❀   ❀   ❀   ❀   ❀

What have I learned in my quest to be an Olympic caliber sculler? I have learned too many things to include in one short book, for sure. Mostly, though, I learned the importance of pursuing excellence in all aspects of life, not only in crew. My goals are now diverse, and my efforts are steadfast in an attempt to maximize all my interests and overcome all the inevitable obstacles that will stand in my way. There will be times when I sink low. The challenge is obviously to rise up from defeat. More significantly, the challenge is to rise from defeat with a broader perspective that teaches us all a valuable lesson: rarely in life do we have anything to lose. No, I do not deny how devastating losing can be, even on a completely practical level. An investor, for instance, can lose all the money to his name with a single investment. Nothing can be more practically devastating. What one must do, however, is maintain a perspective that helps one realize there is always more to life than the losses or victories one activity can supply. The investor who loses his fortune in one transaction must remember there is more to life than money. The athlete who loses after spending his entire existence trying to win one race, must remember there is more to life than a race. There is even more to life than sport. These are hard notions to keep in mind sometimes, but the more we can keep the entire breadth of our lives in perspective, the more rich our lives will become, the better people we will be, and the greater victories we will reap from our defeats.